THE DESIRING SELF

Rooting Pastoral Counseling and Spiritual Direction in Self-Transcendence

Walter E. Conn

PAULIST PRESS
New York/Mahwah, N.J.

ACKNOWLEDGMENTS:

The author thanks the editors of the following journals and books for use of material that originally appeared in different form in their pages: *Counseling and Values, Horizons, Pastoral Psychology, The Way,* and *The New Dictionary of Catholic Spirituality,* ed. Michael Downey (Collegeville, MN: Liturgical Press, 1993).

Library of Congress Cataloging-in-Publication Data:

Conn, Walter E.
    The desiring self : rooting pastoral counseling and spiritual direction in self-transcendence / Walter E. Conn.
        p.   cm.
    Includes bibliographical references and index.
    ISBN 0-8091-3831-X (alk. paper)
    1. Pastoral counseling. 2. Spiritual direction. 3. Self. I. Title.
BV4012.2.C59   1998
253.5–dc21   98-39635
                                                                                CIP

Cover design by Tim McKeen
Interior design by Joseph E. Petta
Typeset in 11/13 Berkeley Oldstyle

Published by Paulist Press
997 Macarthur Boulevard
Mahwah, New Jersey 07430

www.paulistpress.com

Printed and bound in the
United States of America

CONTENTS

DEDICATION

To Joann Wolski Conn, Eileen Flanagan, and Phillip Bennett
of the Neumann College Graduate Program in
Pastoral Counseling, Spiritual Direction, and Spiritual Care

In memory of
Bernard Lonergan

INTRODUCTION

Desire is at the heart of Christian experience. From Augustine's *Confessions* to Thomas Merton's *Seven Storey Mountain*, Christian autobiography has centered on desire. This tradition has emphasized a fundamental distinction in desire: the desire to possess and the desire to give. From Augustine and Merton we learn about concupiscence, but also about the desire to rest in God—not to possess God, but to give oneself fully to God.[1] In lesser literature we read about grasping the truth, possessing the good, gaining justice, having love, but through the classics of the Christian tradition we discover our desire to give ourselves to truth, to the good, to justice, to love, in a word, to God—our desire to dwell in the God who is truth, who is goodness, who is love. Such is the radical meaning of Christian vocation.[2] This book on the desiring self is a study of the self with a heart restless for God.

To a great extent, pastoral counseling and spiritual direction focus on desire. "Only by attending to our desires," writes Philip Sheldrake, "are we able to encounter our deepest self—the image of God within us."[3] Many of our desires are possessive, even obsessive. But only by taking all our desires seriously *as our own* can we distinguish our deepest desires from the superficial, the unhealthy, as well as from instincts and needs, both conscious and unconscious. Such discernment is a central task of pastoral counseling and spiritual direction, an always difficult task because intense feelings are not always deep desires. In our deepest selves we discover

1

that our radical desires are God's desires.[4] In other words, our radical desires are God within us, and thus disclose not only who we ultimately *are* but also, very concretely, who we *ought to be*.[5] Our deepest desire finally is one—an eros of the self for the infinite, an eschatological desire that is never filled but ever deepened by the Desired. To *rest* in God, therefore, is paradoxical: it is to dwell in the dynamic openness of infinite Desire itself.[6]

The self finds itself in a deeply ambiguous situation these days. A modern creation taken for granted by much of philosophy, theology, and psychology, the reality and, indeed, the very possibility of a unitary and coherent self is also denied by some important contemporary authors.[7] My approach understands the self as a unity, but a complex unity-in-tension. Defined by its desire for self-transcendence, this self's very meaning is constituted in its relation to others. Although I have learned from various sources, ancient to contemporary, this book is not an entry in the ongoing cultural debate about the self. The understanding of the self presented here will inevitably be located somewhere on the map of current options, but this book's purpose is primarily constructive and practical—a handbook for pastoral counselors and spiritual directors struggling with the meaning of self in their work, a guidebook for practitioners seeking to find their way through the labyrinth of psychological theories about the self.

There is a widespread misunderstanding that theory is impractical, only for theoreticians. The truth is that theory is for practitioners. Architects, for example, need to understand the physical properties of steel in order to design bridges. Pastoral counselors and spiritual directors need to understand the psychospiritual properties of the self in order to effect development and promote conversion. Unfortunately, the nature of the self has proven more elusive than the nature of steel. This book means to be both theoretical and practical, to present a theoretical understanding of the self of practical import for architects of the soul. Focusing on the self in its desire for transcendence, I will attempt to design several bridges: between psychology and theology, between the self and transcendence, between development and conversion, between pastoral counseling and spiritual direction. And at every point I will try to bridge the theoretical and the practical. This book, then, is an essay in integration—a practical theory of the desiring self.

The psychology-theology connection in pastoral counseling and spiritual direction needs some clarification here at the very beginning. M. Scott Peck has highlighted the significance of this bridging as part of a historical movement "out of an age of excessive specialization into an age of integration."[8] In pastoral counseling's relatively short history, for example, there have been many attempts to make it interdisciplinary by integrating psychology on the one side and either theology, or religion, or spirituality, or Christian faith on the other. All too often, of course, psychology ended up dominating the pastoral counseling partnership.

Pastoral counseling had hardly been established, therefore, when—counterbalancing psychology's strong influence—efforts were begun to distinguish what was distinctively *pastoral* about it. Perhaps the most successful of these efforts has been the specification of context as the feature that distinguishes pastoral counseling precisely as pastoral. This *context* has been identified, for example, both as pastoral care (for example, the parish) and, more generally, as the "moral and religious assumptive world associated with the Judeo-Christian tradition,"[9] that is, the faith that constitutes the caring community. Today, the trend is clearly in the "direction of reaffirming the distinctively religious and theological dimensions of pastoral counseling."[10] Just how this is to be done is not so clear, however. And neither are the central terms of the discussion.

A basic distinction is necessary if we are to appreciate the complexity of the integration issue that Peck rightly emphasizes. We must distinguish between first- and second-order questions, between those questions that are immediately practical and those theoretical questions that have significant practical implications. To designate the full ministry of pastoral care within a Christian community as the proper context of *pastoral* counseling is to respond to the first order, immediately practical issue of assuring the Christian character of counseling: counseling will be pastoral insofar as it is explicitly understood and practiced in the context of the Christian community's ministry of pastoral care. In this practical equation, then, pastoral counseling is related to the context of pastoral care; pastoral counseling is identified as a particular ministry within the full ministry of pastoral care.

As adequate as this response may be to the question of distinguishing pastoral counseling from secular counseling, it implicitly

assumes that counseling is compatible with Christian faith. An alto-
gether different kind of response is necessary if one questions that
very assumption, if one asks the second-order question of whether
counseling really is compatible with Christian faith, whether it
truly is a form of pastoral care. Now the theoretical cat is out of the
bag, for now one is asking whether the psychological foundation of
counseling is consistent with the theological understanding of
Christian faith—or, rather, whether a particular psychological foundation of counseling is consistent with one's particular theological
understanding of Christian faith (for only particular understandings of abstractions like "psychology" and "theology" exist in the
concrete). Now the issue is one of relating (linking or splitting,
integrating or differentiating) interpretations or theories of the
human: critically correlating psychologies and theologies. Some
may relate positively even though others may not. One theology
may deny the possibility of integration with any psychology;
another may not. One psychology may reject the validity of all theology; another may not. Obviously, then, how one understands
"psychology" and "theology" is crucial.

    If, for example, psychology is understood as promoting self-
affirmation, self-fulfillment, or self-realization, and if Christian faith
is understood theologically as demanding self-denial, self-emptying,
or self-surrender, the candidates for integration appear to be radically opposed to each other. But, these are precisely the visions presented by the major psychologies grounding contemporary
counseling and by traditional readings of the Christian gospel. It is
no wonder, then, that the pastoral counseling movement has struggled with the theoretical problem of relating psychology and theology from its beginning to the present day. Is it possible to reconcile
the psychological goal of self-realization with the theological understanding of self-surrender demanded by the gospel, and thus effect a
foundational integration at the very heart of pastoral counseling? A
Christian's decision on whether or not to use psychological ideas
and techniques in the *practice* of the pastoral care we call counseling
will depend on her or his answer to this basic *theoretical* question.
I am convinced that a theory of self-transcendence can not only integrate the goals of self-realization and self-surrender in a single
vision of the human person, but also explicate the intrinsic unity of

authentic psychological and theological interpretations of the self's structured dynamism to reach beyond itself.

While I referred specifically to pastoral counseling in the previous paragraph, the point is also true, *mutatis mutandis,* for spiritual direction. Though spiritual direction is a much older (indeed ancient) form of pastoral care, its relation to psychological theories has become a major issue in recent decades. Early pastoral care in America was actually a Protestant version of spiritual direction. And, as we will see, the best of contemporary pastoral counseling includes the concerns of spiritual direction within it. To the extent that a distinction needs to be made between the two, I specify pastoral counseling as dealing with particular *problems* (developmental and others) in a Christian's life, and spiritual direction as addressing a Christian's radical *desire* for ongoing development and conversion.

My theoretical premise is that the fundamental desire of the self is to transcend itself in relationship: to the world, to others, to God. But only a developed, powerful self has the strength to realize significant transcendence. My approach, therefore, recognizes two focal points in the fundamental human desire: the drive *to be a self,* a center of strength; and the dynamism to *move beyond the self* in relationship. My interpretation of the desiring self will not only include both elements, it will insist on their inextricable connection; the desires to be a self and to reach out beyond the self must always be understood together: separation *and* attachment, independence *and* belonging, autonomy *and* relationship. The self exists only in relationship to the other. This dual desire of the human heart is expressed in the two words of my basic theoretical term, "self-transcendence," and it is the core of what I mean by "the desiring self." Charles Taylor has argued persuasively that the self must always be connected to the good.[11] My interpretation of the desiring self insists that this connection is *intrinsic:* by its nature the self desires to transcend itself, to move beyond itself to the good.

Without an accurate understanding of the self, the meaning of self-transcendence remains vague, leaving pastoral counseling and spiritual direction without an integrated theoretical base, and pastoral counselors and spiritual directors without an effective practical appreciation of their clients' radical desires and possibilities. The understanding of the self presented here must be complex: multidimensional and interdisciplinary. Integrating insights from philosophy and theology as well as psychology, it will be defined in relation to, and include within it, basic meanings of often difficult terms like person, ego, subject, the "I," the "me," identity, consciousness, and the unconscious. To put it briefly, I will be arguing that the self (the person precisely as conscious) is a unity-in-tension—a dynamic, dipolar, dialectical, embodied, first-person reality constituted by consciousness and experienced as "I" (a creating-self at the subject-pole striving for meaning and value in self-transcending relationships) and "me" (a created-self at the object-pole consisting of material, social, and spiritual selves). In this context, the ego will be understood as the unconscious correlative of the self's "I," a unifying drive toward integration, organization, and meaning.

In short, this book is intended as a practical guide through the maze of theories about the self for the Christian who, as a professional helper, is attempting to relate psychological theory to Christian faith. This book should enable the reader to approach any other discussion of the self in a critical and creative way, whatever its perspective may be—psychoanalysis, Jung's analytic psychology, object relations theory, self psychology, transpersonal psychology, or developmental psychology.

I am convinced that an accurate understanding of the desiring self in its journey through development and conversion is necessary for every practitioner of the Christian life. I trust that you will agree, and hope that you will find the following pages of theory eminently practical. In order to demonstrate concretely the practical need for a clear and adequate understanding of the self, we will begin in Chapter 1 with a well-known case study and its conflicting interpretations. Then, after situating the self in the history of American pastoral counseling in Chapter 2, I will construct an understanding of the self in Chapter 3, give it a post-Freudian psychoanalytical context in Chapter 4, and elaborate on it in terms of self-transcendence, the true self, and self-love in Chapter 5. In Chapters 6 and 7, summarizing earlier work,[12] I will consider the self in its development and conversions, and finally, in view of all this, take a second, critical look at the case study in Chapter 8.

The completion of a book is a special occasion to reflect on the gifts that made it possible, and to thank some of the people who offered them. In memory of Bernard Lonergan, I am dedicating this book to my wife, Joann, and to Eileen Flanagan and Phillip Bennett, our friends and colleagues in the Pastoral Counseling, Spiritual Direction, and Spiritual Care Graduate Program at Neumann College, Aston, Pennsylvania. I am also deeply indebted to my colleagues over the years at Catholic Social Services in Chester County, especially Lisa Curran, O.S.F., Bill Kefer, and Anita Mentzer. At Villanova University, I want to thank Sue Toton and Rodger Van Allen for twenty years of warm friendship and support, and Leo Zuckowsky for his care in guiding me through my counseling education. And, at Paulist Press, I am especially grateful to Don Brophy for his patient encouragement.

Chapter 1

Understanding Mary

The meaning of "self" is crucial for pastoral counseling and spiritual direction. But psychologists, philosophers, and theologians use the term "self," as well as "ego" and "person," in so many different ways that confusion is widespread. In order to show in a very concrete way exactly what is at stake for the practitioner, this chapter presents a case study illustrating such confusion. We will first meet Mary, a young woman struggling with her post-conversion Christian faith. Then we will consider two very different interpretations of Mary's experience, rooted in two conflicting understandings of the self. The basic point here is to appreciate the need pastoral counselors and spiritual directors have for a clear and adequate understanding of the self in order to be able to assist their clients in the most effective way possible.

MARY'S STORY

Mary, born in 1950, grew up the oldest of four children in a conventional Christian family. Her parents had met at a state university, married, and moved to a village in a rural area where her father had grown up and had many friends. He was a hard worker and a good provider, but Mary's mother felt isolated, lonely, and frustrated. Mary's arrival about a year into the marriage marked the beginning of an enduring antagonistic relationship with her mother. Mary's father was emotionally closed, and she never felt that she knew him very well. As a little girl Mary spent a lot of time alone in her room, playing records and reading. She never felt good about herself, quarrelled constantly with her mother, and from a very early age entertained thoughts about killing herself. Never comfortable at any of several schools, Mary went off to college at seventeen.

Mary attended a private college in the Midwest for a year, then went to California and enrolled in a big state university, but dropped out of that after a short time, too. She did not go back to school, but stayed close to college campuses, not knowing what she wanted to do with her life, except that she wanted to find truth and meaning, to love and be loved. Mary spent the next few years experimenting with illicit drugs, sex, and the occult. After a failed relationship, an auto crash, a shoplifting arrest, and a suicide attempt, Mary had hit rock bottom. While she was recuperating from her suicide attempt, the Lord began to show her that all her unhappiness resulted from her violation of divine law. Mary's realization was vague at first, but about three weeks after her suicide attempt she had an exceptional spiritual experience on LSD. Though it involved no sense of Jesus Christ as Lord, this experience revealed to Mary that "our only purpose on earth is to worship and glorify the Lord...." After several months of seeking within Eastern religions and the occult for perfect knowledge of a way to God, Mary began to doubt this gnostic approach, and was struck by a passage in 2 Timothy 3: 1-7. This was one of many scriptural references listed in a letter from her younger brother Ron, who had recently become a Christian. Mary, then twenty-two, was "convicted of sin." Ron's unexpected arrival home for Christmas a few days later led to Mary's decision to "believe in Jesus Christ and follow him."

After her conversion, Mary had a series of devastating experiences in various small Christian communities. She also became obsessed with the idea of finding a husband, and was dismissed from one community as a result of her declared but unrequited love of a member she felt God meant her to marry. This rejection was particularly painful because Mary had experienced very positive relationships with other community members. Elders of other communities found Mary unsubmissive to authority, and she felt generally miserable as she wandered from one community to another for some two years.

Mary finally found a community that seemed very promising, but after a short time Harry, one of the community's original members, returned after a falling-away. Mary and Harry shared a history of rejection and a great need for relationship. Mary became more and more involved with Harry, and less and less with the community and its ministry. Within four months Mary and Harry were married, but the union was an immediate disaster, as Harry soon turned from Jesus to drugs and other women. Yet the marriage dragged on (and off) for three very difficult years before Mary finally was able to let go, accepting that the Lord was absolving her of her marriage commitment.

The divorce was finalized about the time Mary gave birth to her second child, and as soon as she was able to travel Mary returned with her children to her parents' home, where she met a loving welcome. This put Mary in proximity again to her earlier unrequited love, and hope for possibilities in that direction was rekindled. Mary was particularly excited that her search for a new church had led her to a pastor who was a good friend of the fellow's pastor. She felt a great need to settle the question. In general, Mary felt a strong desire for a deeper relationship with the Lord and for a purpose worth committing herself to—if not a happy marriage, perhaps a form of God's work like Christian education—but she also recognized a real need for a greater source of self-worth.

FOWLER'S INTERPRETATION

Mary's story is featured prominently in James Fowler's *Stages of Faith*.[1] Fowler reports that over the next three years Mary's life moved in a much more positive direction, with a significant increase in her sense of self-worth and happiness. But we will leave her story where it was at the end of the last paragraph, as that is the point where Fowler's interview ends and his analysis begins. The present summary, of course, lacks the richness of detail and verbatim of Fowler's lengthy interview report. Fowler introduced Mary to his readers in order to illustrate the various dimensions of the structural stages in his faith development theory. He found Mary's story especially interesting because of her conversion experience. Fowler's analysis focuses on the years following Mary's conversion, and locates her in the third of his six stages—Synthetic-Conventional faith. In the following paragraphs we will consider each category of Fowler's analysis very briefly in order to see why he characterized Mary's faith as Stage 3. Fowler's categories aim at uncovering *how* one "faiths," not the content of one's beliefs. Later, in Chapter 6, we will examine all of Fowler's faith stages in the context of fully personal development.

Of his seven analytic categories, Fowler begins with *Locus of Authority*. Here Fowler inquires about where Mary turned for guidance in her decisions, for approval in her beliefs and values. He looks first at Mary's pre-conversion years, when she seemed oriented to the conventionally held countercultural values of the sixties. When these failed for her, Mary adopted for a while what Fowler calls a stubborn intellectuality. He suggests that these years (17-22) can be characterized in terms of a counterdependent, anti-establishment stance, neither reflective, systematic, nor critical. Mary's first positive relation to authority occurs in her reference to 2 Timothy 3: 1-7, early in her conversion experience. Here, characteristically, Mary was attracted by a subjectively meaningful passage without any critical attention to its textual, historical, or theological context. Also, and again characteristically, the passage's power for Mary was connected to her brother Ron, who became her most dependable guide in discovering God's will. Ron's influence was the strongest, but there were also other members of the various Christian communities who shared authority for Mary in interpreting God's will, Mary's supreme external locus of authority. Mary's locus of authority seems most clearly described by Stage 3: "Consensus of valued groups and in personally worthy representatives of belief-value traditions." In her countercultural stance Mary had moved beyond Stage 2 "incumbents of authority roles," but she just as clearly had not yet advanced to a Stage 4 locus of authority internalized in her own critically informed personal judgment.

Fowler next considers Mary's *Form of World Coherence*—to what degree was she reflective, concerned about internal consistency, and critically self-conscious in her faith? He suggests that Mary's world coherence inhered in two basic images of God: the God who gives guidance ("I felt that God showed me that I was going to marry a certain brother at that house") and the God who rescues ("The Lord never once forsook me, he was really faithful to me").

While Mary credited God for guidance in many of her decisions, she never held God accountable when these turned out disastrously. The patterns of Mary's images of God went beyond the "Episodic" and "Narrative-Dramatic" forms of Stages 1 and 2, but did not yet form the conceptually mediated explicit system of Stage 4. Mary's pattern was the unquestioned *tacit* "system" of felt meanings mediated by images characteristic of Stage 3: God guides, things go wrong, God rescues.

Fowler turns next to Mary's *Bounds of Social Awareness*—what persons or groups were significant for her faith? Fowler's answer is that Mary's world was limited almost exclusively to "the Lord" and the members of the small communities with whom she had face-to-face interpersonal relationships. Mary's story included virtually no references to social institutions, or to the class, race, ethnic, and ideological differences they involve. Mary is clearly beyond Stage 2, family of origins limits, but just as clearly is not a Stage 4 member of a self-reflective ideological community. Again, Stage 3, with its "composite of groups in which one has interpersonal relationships," best characterizes Mary's bounds of social awareness.

The next focus of attention is Mary's *Symbolic Function*—the terms, images, and metaphors she uses in referring to the transcendent. Are they intended as literal or metaphorical, as one-dimensional or multi-leveled and multivalent? Are the symbols recognized as symbols, have they been questioned for conceptually stable meanings? At times Mary seems to distinguish between symbols like "the Lord," "God," "Jesus Christ," and "the Spirit," but she usually uses "the Lord" to refer to all the persons of the trinity. "The Lord" is clearly a powerfully emotional symbol for Mary, but it seems just as clear that she has no explicitly delineated *concept* of God derived from critical reflection on the many dimensions of meaning of "the Lord." Fowler sees Mary's Symbolic Function as beyond the magical-numinous, one-dimensional, literal qualities of Stages 1 and 2, but not yet possessing Stage 4's conceptual, critical distance from symbolic meanings. Her faith is characterized by Stage 3's evocative power of multidimensional symbols.

Since Fowler's three remaining categories—*Form of Logic, Perspective Taking,* and *Moral Judgment*—are based on the theories of Jean Piaget, Robert Selman, and Lawrence Kohlberg, which we will be considering later, our treatment here will be very brief. Fowler thinks that while Mary's cognitive ability, or Form of Logic, is clearly beyond what Piaget calls concrete operations, since she can reflect on her life and generalize about it, it is only at the early formal (or elementary abstract) level of operations characteristic of Stage 3, as Mary manifests no critical distance on her self or her world view. Mary's Perspective Taking follows the same Stage 3 pattern. She consistently used the interpersonal form—her attempt to see things from her mother's point of view, for example—but she did not regularly enter the perspectives of others on themselves or on her viewpoint. The absence of mutuality and a third-person viewpoint in her Perspective Taking also limited Mary to the Stage 3 Moral Judgment of "interpersonal expectations and concordance." As Fowler sees it, Mary has only a fragile and provisional sense of self, which holds together—but in a real sense is a prisoner of—the perceived evaluations and images significant others have of her. Mary has no transcendent "cognitive ego" that can put her reflective sense of self together in a critical way with her assessments of others and of others' evaluations of her.

And this is the problem Fowler has with Mary's conversion. While Fowler is convinced that Mary's experience was a genuine conversion, he understands it as seriously limited by the weakness in Mary's sense of her self at the time. For this interpretation, Fowler adds Erik Erikson's psychosocial ages of the life cycle to the structural-developmental perspective. He finds in Mary's life story—especially in her relationship with her mother—suggestions of problems at the early childhood periods of trust, autonomy, initiative, and competence that set Mary up for the development of an angry, negative identity in adolescence, a negative identity reinforced by the countercultural movement of the 1960s. In the conversion following Mary's rock-bottom experience, Fowler sees "previously scattered and ambiguous vectors of fidelity" finding a focus in Jesus Christ.[2] At the same time, Mary was promised that her negative identity and life patterns could be left behind, as she turned and submitted her will to the will of the Lord. But, says Fowler, "Mary was a new Christian without a church" in which her new identity in Christ could take shape. Rather, by encouraging not the transformation but the negation of Mary's willful self, the groups Mary lived in after her conversion only helped to continue her experience of psychological and spiritual violence. By demanding the denial of a weak and fragile self, they undercut whatever potential

Mary had, thus preventing growth in either the structuring of her faith or the strength of her identity. In Fowler's view, Mary's conversion process was short-circuited by the strategy of obliterating her past life. What Mary needed was a healing recapitulation of the earlier stages of her faith in light of her new relationship with God. Such prayerful and imaginative continuation of her conversion process could have supported a growth in identity and faith that Mary could bring to intimacy and ministry, rather than search for in them.

FORD-GRABOWSKY'S INTERPRETATION

Having presented a summary of Mary's story and Fowler's interpretation, we turn now to another interpretation from a quite different perspective. In the context of a critique of Fowler's faith development theory, Mary Ford-Grabowsky offers a counter-interpretation of Mary's story based on what she considers a more expansive, "holistic" concept of person.[3] In contrast to what she calls Fowler's *ego* psychology, Ford-Grabowsky employs Jung's psychological understanding of the *self* and Hildegard of Bingen's theological concept of the *inner person.*

As Ford-Grabowsky presents Jung, the self is the subject of the total psyche, conscious and unconscious, whereas the ego is the center only of consciousness. The self is a "transcendental postulate," ultimately unknowable, expressed in dream symbolism as a mandala or as one's ideal personality. In addition to the collective unconscious, the self has a personal unconscious, made up not only of repressed and forgotten materials but also of two archetypal constructs, the negative shadow and the contrasexual anima/animus. The self is a *coniunctio oppositorum,* in which a healthy tension between polarities like unique/universal and unitemporal/eternal is maintained by a uniting symbol of the transcendental function.

Hildegard, in Ford-Grabowsky's presentation, distinguishes between the outer person and the inner person, reflecting the various dichotomies of the spiritual life in Pauline theology. While the outer person is characterized by blindness and deafness, a fleshly intellect, pride, resistance to grace, obliviousness to the demands of justice, and selfishness or willfulness, the inner person is marked by special faculties of seeing and hearing, a spiritual intellect, humility, openness to grace, a sensitivity to justice, and selflessness or a desire to do God's will. But, at the bottom line, the inner person's life of faith is what distinguishes it from the outer person. Ford-Grabowsky calls the inner person the Christian self, to distinguish it from the Jungian self.

In contrast to Jung and Hildegard, Fowler is seen as focusing on the ego and, along with it, cognition, consciousness, and positivity, while neglecting the self, affect, the unconscious, and negativity. In summary outline, then, according to this view, Fowler concentrates on the ego, Jung introduces the fuller reality of the self, and Hildegard goes beyond both by shifting the focus to the Pauline inner person or Christian self. In this context, Ford-Grabowsky's key point is that since only Hildegard's inner person experiences Christian faith, and since Fowler considers only the ego and not the inner person, "then Fowler must be studying some other phenomenon than faith, and mistakenly naming it 'faith.'"[4] In her view, moreover, while Fowler's first four stages concentrate on structures of the ego, his fifth and sixth stages inadvertently shift the focus to the self. As a result, Fowler brings together in his faith development theory two different lines of development—ego and self—that, according to Ford-Grabowsky, are "logically incapable of combination."[5]

Now, in this context, when Ford-Grabowsky looks at Mary, she sees not one conversion, but two: a conversion from ego to self, and a conversion from self to Christian self. In this view, Mary, as a result of her spiritual experience while taking LSD, was transformed from an unbeliever into a believer. Through this transformation she attained religious faith, but not Christian faith, as her belief was in a monistic, not triune, God. This conversion represents movement from Fowler's ego to Jung's self, but not yet from Jung's self to Hildegard's Christian self. Ford-Grabowsky interprets Mary's next several months as a journey of the Jungian self, a gnostic search for perfect knowledge of the God within.

Mary's second conversion, from self to Christian self, centered on her experience in reading 2 Timothy 3: 1-7 and on conversations with her brother Ron. She now believed in the triune God of Christian faith, God both immanent and transcendent. According to Ford-Grabowsky, Mary's double conversion illustrates Hildegard's view of the dynamics of faith: as an egocentric outer person,

Mary was incapable of faith, but as a transcended inner person she became capable of faith. Mary's "progress along the ego/self/Christian self axis was accompanied by progress from unbelief to belief in God, and from belief in God to belief in the trinity."[6]

Looking at Mary's post-conversion life, Ford-Grabowsky thinks that Fowler, regarding Mary as a case of arrested development in faith, fails to appreciate the life of grace that was unfolding within and bringing her closer to Christ. In Ford-Grabowsky's estimation, Mary's post-conversion life exemplified two key factors in Hildegard's understanding of the Christian self: Christian faith and Christian character. Ford-Grabowsky sees Mary's faith as strong and unshakable because even the most bitter suffering during her marriage did not make her doubt the Lord's goodness and faithfulness. As evidence of Mary's growth in Christian character, Ford-Grabowsky cites examples of Mary's imitation of Christ's virtues: fortitude, obedience, forgiveness, understanding, love. For instance, Ford-Grabowsky sees fortitude, one of the gifts of the Holy Spirit, in Mary's remarkable endurance in her commitment to both Christ and the church despite the emotional abuse she suffered from church members, and in her struggle to stay faithful to a marriage that became impossibly difficult. In short, Ford-Grabowsky perceives in Mary "neither the egocentricity of the 'outer person,' nor the sub-Christian beliefs of the Jungian self"; Mary exemplifies, rather, the "inner person" alive in Christ.[7]

Now, according to Ford-Grabowsky's interpretation of Fowler's perspective, "Fowler sees Mary as a case of retarded development in faith who occupies only stage 3 while she ought chronologically to be at stage 4."[8] This happens, in Ford-Grabowsky's view, because Fowler confuses the distinction between ego development (Stages 1-4) and spiritual development (Stages 5-6), and tries to integrate the two in one theory of faith development. Because of this confusion, Ford-Grabowsky claims that Mary can be shown to be simultaneously at (ego) Stage 3 and (spiritual) Stage 5 of faith development—an internal contradiction. To Ford-Grabowsky's eye, Mary's *self*, actualized by grace, exhibits the characteristics of Fowler's Stage 5, while her fragmented *ego* looks like Stage 3. Actually, as she says, Ford-Grabowsky thinks that the characteristics of Fowler's Stage 5 (knowing one's shadow, a willingness to surrender defenses, a knowledge of the opposites, a coherence of the imperative and the indicative in the moral life, and a relatedness to being) are qualities of Jungian self-actualization. Thus Fowler's theory tracks the development of the ego and of the Jungian self, but not of the Christian self whose faith and character Mary exemplifies. To underscore the logical flaw she perceives in Fowler's theory, Ford-Grabowsky suggests that perhaps Fowler needs to add a seventh stage to his theory in order to account for the development of the Christian self possible with grace. She immediately points out, of course, that Mary would then—absurdly—be at Stage 3 (ego), Stage 5 (self), and Stage 7 (Christian self)! For Ford-Grabowsky, then, Fowler's case study of Mary both exposes his limited concept of person and thus of faith, and at the same time presents a powerful example of growth in authentic Christian faith.

CONCLUSION

We have now seen two very different views of Mary's development and conversion. While much more could be said about these two perspectives on Mary, and especially about Ford-Grabowsky's interpretation of Fowler, it is not the purpose of this chapter to argue for one or the other, or even to referee the dispute. But this is the place to stress one key point. Whether or not Ford-Grabowsky is correct in her judgment that Fowler's concept of the person is limited, I think she has put her finger on a basic problem underlying the difference in their interpretations of Mary when she points to the concept of person.

What separates Fowler and Ford-Grabowsky here is one of the most complex and difficult issues in psychology, philosophy, and theology. Terms like "ego," "self," and "person" are used regularly by authors in these fields without any commonly accepted definitions or understandings of the terms. In the case of the present authors, we have Ford-Grabowsky bringing peculiarly Jungian meanings of ego and self to Fowler's completely different context of developmental psychology, where the terms have other meanings. Moreover, Ford-Grabowsky's use of Jungian categories appears to have more of a theological than a psychological purpose. For no sooner does she introduce the Jungian *self* as a more comprehensive view of the person than the *ego* which she attributes to

Fowler, than she makes the next move to Hildegard's Pauline *inner person,* or *Christian self,* because the Jungian *self* is inadequate, in her view, to the graced reality of Christian faith. Ford-Grabowsky takes exception to Fowler's theory of faith development, therefore, more for theological than for psychological reasons. Essentially, although she contrasts the Jungian *self* favorably to what she calls Fowler's *ego,* she finds from her theological perspective that neither psychological approach is capable of doing justice to the person graced in Christian faith. For that, in her theological view, only Hildegard's Pauline *inner person,* or *Christian self* will do: a theological, not a psychological, understanding of the person. In other words, with Fowler we have a strongly psychological approach to faith development and conversion, while Ford-Grabowsky offers a heavily theological approach from her own understanding of Christian faith, a reality she sees as beyond the ability of any psychological theory to deal with adequately. Ford-Grabowsky makes her theological leaning clear when she explains her preference for Hildegard's inner person over Fowler's outer person (ego) as the subject of faith by reminding us that Hildegard's inner person is biblical, anchored in Paul.[9]

Clearly, these sharply conflicting interpretations of Mary carry significant practical implications for diagnosis and care. And they indicate that every interpretation of a client's history and present condition will be crucially influenced by the interpreter's understanding of the nature of the human person. Practice, in other words, is inevitably influenced by theory in a very fundamental way. It is paramount, therefore, that the practitioner possess the most adequate theoretical understanding of the human person possible, in order to make an accurate interpretation of any client's situation. The purpose of this book is to construct, for the sake of good practice, such an understanding of the human person, or, as I shall say, of the *self.* We shall be returning to Mary in due course, but we turn now in the next chapter to the American historical context of this attempt to provide pastoral counselors and spiritual directors with a theory of self-transcendence: the radical desire of the self for both autonomy and relationship, the dual desire to be a self and to reach out beyond the self to world, others, and God.

Chapter 2

From Self-Denial to Self-Realization: An American History

While pastoral counseling as we know it today is essentially a post-World War II phenomenon, it first appeared earlier in the century with the blossoming of psychology, and it can claim American ancestors in philosophical psychology all the way back to the Mayflower. In this chapter we will first review the developing interplay between psychology and theology as presented in E. Brooks Holifield's history of pastoral counseling in America. Then we will survey the approaches major authors in the modern pastoral counseling movement have taken to the psychology-theology question, noting hints of a solution in terms of self-transcendence. This will be followed by an examination of the influential contemporary position developed by Howard Clinebell. Finally, drawing on resources from these approaches, I will present a brief summary of an integrated vision of pastoral counseling for self-transcendence— a vision that, by focusing on psychology and theology as different interpretations of the single desire for self-transcendence, reveals the problem of reconciling them as a false one.

IDEALS OF THE SELF THROUGH FOUR CENTURIES

Following the direction of his book's subtitle, *From Salvation to Self-Realization,* Holifield details the development of pastoral counseling in America as a succession of changing ideals of the self: from self-denial to self-love, from self-love to self-culture, from self-culture to self-mastery, and from self-mastery to self-realization, with the last being understood at first as occurring within a trustworthy culture and later as countercultural.[1] We will now follow the historical trail of these ideals of the self, with their apparent shift from the theological ideal of self-denial to the psychological ideal of self-realization.

Self-Denial

Sin was a central focus of religious life in seventeenth-century America. Whatever its interpretation within the different traditions, sin and salvation from sin was the paramount concern of pastoral care, the cure of souls. Also common to the various traditions was a hierarchical view of reality reaching from God down to the lowliest creature, a view that not only included society and the self within the cosmos but saw the self (soul) and society as themselves hierarchical microcosms. The pastor had a place within the social hierarchy, and his task was caring for the welfare of souls conceived as monarchies troubled by rebellion of the self.[2] While the "soul" was an incorruptible spiritual substance created directly by God, for seventeenth-century clerical psychologists, the "self" meant self-centeredness, willful egocentricity. Thus selfhood, rather than a positive psychological state to be realized, was a negative, idolatrous condition to be overcome by self-denial. In the hierarchical soul, spiritual growth meant a process of sanctification, and while this process was empowered by supernatural grace, hierarchical continuity allowed for the pastoral application of rational methods of interpretation and persuasion toward overcoming sinful disorder. Aspects of Mary's story suggest that this vision continues today.

The eighteenth century saw a continuation of the assumptions about hierarchical authority, a supernatural order, and the pastoral use of rational method. But the spiritual upheaval of the Great Awakening was the occasion for some serious reconsideration of the hierarchy of the soul's faculties. The question was not one of simply reordering the hierarchy of intellect, will, and affections, but of reconceiving the very structure of the soul. While the anti-revivalist Old Lights held to a hierarchy in which understanding was "higher" in importance and value and affections were "lower," the revivalist New Lights viewed the soul in terms of surface and depth, wherein the understanding may be of preliminary importance, but is superficial in comparison with the deep affections. In fact, Jonathan Edwards sought to overcome the dichotomy of the hierarchical view by insisting on a unified sensible knowledge that combined understanding and will, an apprehension infused with affection that engaged the whole person. It was from this deep sensible knowledge, in Edwards' view, that religious affections flowed.[3]

Since everyone agreed that the main function of private pastoral care was discernment, or the diagnosis of one's spiritual state, the different views of the soul and the interrelationship of its faculties raised a crucial pastoral question. Convinced of the need to penetrate below surface appearances to the soul's deep affections, New Light revivalists encouraged the long, agonizing period of inner turmoil necessary for rebirth of the soul. Rebirth was an arduous, wrenching experience because it required the breaking of the proud will, the suppression of the sinfully assertive self. Such conversion required self-despair and an intense "conviction of sin." In this context, the character of Mary's conversion and willfulness seem very familiar. The Old Light ministers, on the other hand, saw God working in more gentle, gradual ways, and judged conversion more by the fruits of a holy life than by the feelings of a dramatic rebirth. Their pastoral style thus stressed comfort more than challenge.[4]

Self-Love

While most pastors of both persuasions still agreed on the necessity of self-denial, the eighteenth century also saw a growing infatuation with the self, first among liberal ministers, then even among some Old Calvinist theologians. Distinguished from selfishness, self-love and the desire for happiness began to be seen as a means for encouraging sinners to prepare themselves for saving grace. Though followers of Edwards saw no middle ground between total selfishness and total selflessness, the historical tide was against them, and self-love was soon established as a principle of pastoral care.[5]

Where eighteenth-century pastors could not agree on whether understanding or affections should be given priority, early nineteenth-century ministers, drawing from theology and psychology, hit upon a solution in the ideal of a tripartite balance of reason, sentiment, and will. With sin now seen more as a personal act of will than as a status, the goal of pastoral conversation was to move the will to a decision for faithfulness through a judicious use of both rational analysis ("affable and affectionate interrogation") and sympathetic silence. Thus despite an ideal of inner harmony, hierarchic thinking still prevailed and promoted priority of will, not inner equality.[6]

Self-Culture

The way to assure that the will would govern a balance within the self was the formation of habits toward self-control. Since virtue and self-love were no longer seen as opposed to each other, emphasis on habit and virtue soon extended self-love into an antebellum ideal of self-culture. Understood as the nurture and enhancement of one's actual faculties, self-culture did not possess its own criterion of values, but required the subordination of the self to God's will, and thus was seen in continuity with salvation.[7] In Mary's small Christian communities great importance was given to the virtue of obedience.

Self-Mastery

Sometime after the Civil War, writes Holifield, pastoral theologians "lost their sense of balance." And by the turn of the century the ideal of inner harmony among faculties had given way to an acute interest in the vitality of human nature. Fascination with "nature" and "power" led first to a religious appropriation of the language of science and technology. As evolutionary theory emphasized conflict and struggle, the ethical affirmation of self-love and development of character subtly shifted from an ideal of self-culture to one of self-mastery: the moral warrior realized ideals through conflict. Such Christianity called for a "muscular minister."[8]

But toward the end of the century the assimilation of the New Psychology into liberal theology effected yet another shift in emphasis: from activity to receptivity. William James was a strong proponent of will and habit, but he also appreciated the importance of repose and relaxation, and he focused attention on the energies of the wider subliminal or subconscious self as the source of salvation, and on the necessity of surrendering the conscious ego to these subconscious energies. This psychology, as well as Freudian and other interpretations of the unconscious, found a perfect niche in the new liberal restatement of theology in terms of personal relations, which emphasized communion with an immanent Person more than conformity to God's transcendent will. The New Psychology was warmly welcomed by a theology that located God's activity within the subjectivity of faithful Christians. Self-mastery remained the Christian ideal—the building of character through the overcoming of powerful vitalities within the self.[9]

Self-Realization

Holifield characterizes pastoral counseling in the first half of the twentieth century, when America's love affair with psychology really got serious, through the ideal of self-realization, an ideal understood first in terms of adjustment, later in terms of insight.

The ethic of self-realization was initially an expansion of the ethic of character, not a justification of the uninhibited expression of natural desires. The possibility of self-realization, wrote John Dewey, lay in discovering "that special form of character, of self, which includes and transforms all special desires." Because the self was commonly understood to be an intrinsically social reality, self-realization was seen as possible only in relation to other selves, and might even require the sacrifice of "separate" selfhood. Rather than being anti-institutional, such a social conception of self-realization included service to social institutions as a necessary element. This notion of self-realization fitted nicely, therefore, with the other prevailing idea that the self had to be continually adjusting to a changing natural and social environment. As promoted by Dewey, however, this adjustment was no passive subordination to the environment, but an active engagement that transformed both the environment and the self. Only from such adjusting engagement with the world did self-realization emerge.[10]

As powerful as Dewey's influence had been, the attractiveness of the metaphor of adjustment was beginning to fade by the mid-1930s, and pastoral theologians were ready for a new image to guide their work. By 1939, with the publication of Rollo May's *Art of Counseling,* the metaphor of "insight" had assumed center stage in a new play that after the Second World War would become the pastoral counseling movement we know today.[11]

For May, who saw human life marked by a conflict between freedom and determination, every counseling problem held moral implications, but his psychoanalytic commitment rejected as superficial any appeal to conscious decision. Believing with Alfred Adler that one who understood truly would probably act rightly, May saw the task of counseling as offering interpretations that would lead to insight—not simply rational knowledge, but an understanding that included a capacity to trust reality.[12]

From the theological angle, the transition from adjustment to insight was promoted by the critique of culture made by Paul Tillich and the Niebuhrs. For one did not recommend adjustment to cultural and social institutions that stood in constant need of critique, lest they become idols. With the theological realists, then, the notion of sin shifted from a false adaptation to the divine to an idolatrous relationship to cultural values. Counseling would work toward trusting insight to transcend this idolatry. But in criticizing culture, theological realism subverted not only adjustment but also the concept of self-realization attached to it. With those for whom it was to remain an ideal, therefore, self-realization had to be redefined as a transcending of social convention, lest it become itself an idol.[13] And thus it was redefined—some would say, with a vengeance—during the post-war years. Among the leading psychological theorists of the new version of self-realization Holifield highlights Carl Rogers, Karen Horney, and Erich Fromm, social critics who viewed self-realization as an ethic of individual growth, against the bureaucratic impositions of social institutions.

Erich Fromm was perhaps the most influential of the critics of mass culture, with his combination of psychoanalysis and social-economic critique. Pastoral theologians found his affirmation of the religious quest and rational conscience reassuring, while appreciating his powerful criticisms of authoritarian religion and ethics. Pastoral theologians also found Karen Horney's criticism of Western competitiveness as a generator of anxiety very convincing. This critique of mass culture and its conventions fitted in perfectly with a simultaneous revolt against moralism in ethics and theology. Although many theologians in this movement had little use for the ideal of self-realization, Paul Tillich was able to use it to bring together the social and theological critiques in a powerful synthesis of human and divine imperatives: self-realization was the human precondition of obedience to the divine command to love.[14]

Fromm, Horney, and other theorists of self-realization distinguished between a "real" self and a public self. Fromm affirmed the truly human self behind the pseudo public self as the organism's inner drive to actualize its potential toward growth and integration. Horney focused her criticism on the neurotic "idealized image" the self created in response to anxiety. This moralistic idealized image subjected the self to "the tyranny of the should" and trapped it in a "pride system" veiling self-contempt and alienation. Only the real self could move toward autonomy, growth, and fulfillment.[15]

Carl Rogers, with his emphasis on acceptance, was a "natural" for this context of trust in the self's capacity for growth and of distrust of authoritarian institutions and moralism.[16] A counselor's unconditional acceptance of even the most unacceptable impulses in clients, as Rogers explained in his 1942 *Counseling and Psychotherapy*,[17] would give relief from moralistic expectations and institutional impositions, and would open the way to client self-acceptance and self-realization.[18] This conviction, infused with a liberal Protestant spirit and an optimism about human nature with its ethical concern for self-realization, guided Rogers' early efforts at "nondirective" counseling. Responding more to feelings than to content, the counselor's acceptance sought the client's free release of feelings that would lead to insight, a new perception of inner impulses. Such insight would foster self-acceptance, leading to growth.[19] So deep was Rogers' respect for the client's feelings that, in his 1951 *Client-Centered Therapy,* he dropped even clarification of feelings by the counselor, because it implied the disrespectful assumption that the counselor knew the client's feelings better than the client did.[20] Instead, he emphasized the importance of adopting the client's "frame-of-reference" through empathy, the skill Rollo May had seen as the key to good counseling. The counselor's empathic, nonjudgmental attitude would encourage the client's inherent tendency to self-actualization as a social person.[21] Rogers' understanding of acceptance and self-realization, set within the post-war milieu of cultural critique and antimoralism, defines the context for our consideration of the period's major authors in pastoral counseling: Seward Hiltner, Carroll Wise, Paul

Johnson, and Wayne Oates. Holifield's fine history has brought us from seventeenth-century self-denial through self-love, self-culture, and self-mastery to twentieth-century self-realization. In the next section we follow the career of this ambivalent and ambiguous concept in the specific field of pastoral counseling.

SELF-REALIZATION IN MODERN PASTORAL COUNSELING

Seward Hiltner

Certain books define a field during a critical period. Seward Hiltner's *Pastoral Counseling,* published in 1949, performed that task for a generation of pastoral counselors. While Hiltner understood pastoral counseling within the broad aims of the church, he saw its special aim as "the attempt by a pastor to help people help themselves through the process of gaining understanding of their inner conflicts."[22]

In order to define his own general perspective on counseling, Hiltner specified four different views of human nature.[23] First was the social-adjustment view then dominant among secular counselors: An individual's problem is the result of an unsatisfactory adjustment to society. While admitting some truth to this view, Hiltner saw it as a superficial view that could be detrimental to counseling. A second view of human nature that Hiltner judged as gaining in strength among counselors was the inner-release view. Represented in very different ways by Freud, Jung, Rank, Horney, and Rogers, this view posits, beyond an individual's ability to adjust to society, a deep inner need that demands release. As sympathetic as Hiltner is with the more adequate versions of this view, he feels that more is needed—a more that takes the form of an objective ethics. This third view, then, asserts a criterion of basic human (not merely biological) needs, for example, fellowship, whose fulfillment are demanded by the essential core of human nature. A Christian sees this objective ethical character of the human condition as created and supported by God. From this Christian theological view, positive potentialities of personality are seen as having their source in Divine Grace, not as futile sparks in a dark universe. This last Christian perspective is broad and deep enough to include an appreciation of the necessary strengths of the other views as well as a recognition of their limitations.

In terms of method, Hiltner summarizes his approach in five points.[24] 1) The counseling process focuses on the parishioner's situation and feelings about it; 2) the pastor aims at understanding those feelings and communicating that understanding; 3) the pastor helps to clarify conflict in feelings; 4) the counseling relationship includes special freedoms for the parishioner (for example, from inappropriate moral judgment) as well as certain limitations (for example, the pastor gives help toward self-help, not answers or directions); 5) the process should include explicit consolidation of insights and clarification gained, in an attempt to enlarge the parishioner's perspective.

For Hiltner, of course, all this is done within a context of depth psychology that includes three basic assumptions.[25] 1) All conduct has meaning; 2) this meaning is both conscious and unconscious; 3) growth results from the constructive handling of conflict, not from its absence.

It is possible, in all of this, to see not only the Rogerian approach assumed into a theological context, but also—especially in the Christian version of objective ethics—an understanding of self-realization moving in the definite direction of self-transcendence (though the term itself is not used).

Carroll Wise

Carroll Wise continued the Rogerian influence on pastoral counseling with an emphasis, in his 1951 *Pastoral Counseling: Its Theory and Practice,* on the need for an attitude on the part of the counselor of neither approval nor disapproval, but of acceptance.[26] Wise even took this attitude beyond Rogers and Hiltner, however, because he realized that when acceptance expresses a counselor's genuine feelings it can lead to a truly creative relationship, which he affirmed as the essential therapeutic element.

The immediate function of the counseling relationship, in Wise's view, is the strengthening of the self, which cannot face its conflicts alone. Thus, in addition to acceptance, a second key quality of the counseling relationship is freedom, which encourages a person to become an autonomous, self-determining agent with his or her own freedom to engage spontaneously in creative work and human relationships. The third quality of the counseling relationship that Wise highlights is mutuality, which keeps a counselor *with* a person, neither ahead nor behind. Mutuality gives both parties the experience of growing together in insight and understanding. For Wise, then, the acceptance, freedom, and mutuality of relationship all add up to the conclusion that the essence of counseling is communication, the conveying of experience in terms of its meaning—meaning that invariably involves pain, suffering, and other emotional wounds.[27]

Like Rogers, too, Wise sees insight as the goal of counseling— insight that includes perception of relationships in previously known facts, the acceptance of self, and the possibility of choice. Insight, of course, is an emotional grasp of one's self and one's conflicts, not to be confused with intellectual explanation. Insight, for Wise, is the result of an emotional relationship that permits the communication of life experience, the release of negative feelings, and the growth of positive ones. Insight involves grasping oneself as a whole being at the center of personality with one's meanings and values; it includes seeing oneself in relationship to other persons; and it also extends to reaching out beyond one's finite dimensions to the larger universe, to God. Insight, then, in the other words of this book's thesis, is the real possibility of self-transcendence, the overcoming of egocentricity that, as Wise explains, makes prayer in the dominant Christian mood possible: "Thy will be done."[28]

Paul Johnson

The theme of relationship highlighted by Carroll Wise was continued in a major way from the viewpoint of interpersonal psychology in Paul Johnson's 1953 *Psychology of Pastoral Care*. Relationships of mutual appreciation are the key to the pastoral vocation, in Johnson's view. Such relationships involve trusting perception, empathy, and communication.[29]

Johnson developed his pastoral view of relationships from an interpersonal psychology based on seven axioms: 1) persons are central; 2) every person confronts other persons in interactive relationships; 3) motives respond to significant persons; 4) goals are valued by persons; 5) values multiply in sharing; 6) spontaneity is creative;

7) persons grow through love.[30] In this interpersonal context Johnson defines pastoral care as a "religious ministry to individual persons in dynamic relationships, arising from insight into essential needs and mutual discovery of potentialities for spiritual growth."[31]

As may be apparent from the foregoing, Johnson was at this time in complete agreement with the Rogerian nondirective approach. He proposed the label "responsive counseling" simply to stress the active role of the counselor in nondirective counseling. The responsive counselor is oriented to the person, to the relationship, and to God, the creator of all true growth. So, while self-realization is at the heart of Johnson's perspective on the person ("the greatest thing about a person is his capacity to grow and outgrow"), it is a self-realization intrinsically defined by an interpersonal context of relationship. By insisting that self-realization occurs only in relationships, Johnson is insisting that self-realization is what in this book we are calling self-transcendence.[32]

Wayne Oates

The title of Wayne Oates' 1951 *The Christian Pastor* clues us to expect a significantly different orientation. While strongly influenced by psychology and by Rogerian counseling in particular, Oates was deeply rooted in the Christian church of his rural southern culture. Beyond the pastor's personal influence, Oates emphasized the symbolic influence the pastor has by reason of the way the pastor's role and function have seeped deeply into the consciousness of Christians over centuries. The pastor symbolizes Father, Son, and Holy Spirit as emissary of the church. Thus, not surprisingly, *The Christian Pastor* is a book on total pastoral care, with only one of eight chapters devoted to the subdivision of "Pastoral Counseling and Psychotherapy." As much as he appreciated the importance and necessity of psychology for the ministry, Oates did not give blanket endorsement to the notion of self-realization as the goal of pastoral counseling: "The central objective of all *pastoral* care and personal counseling is that 'Christ be formed' in the personality of the individuals who seek help."[33]

Oates distinguishes the counseling process into five major phases: 1) preparatory; 2) relaxation and rapport; 3) listening and exploration; 4) reconstruction and guidance; and 5) follow-up and experimentation. The goal of the third phase, clearly influenced by Rogers, is that the person achieve insight into his or her difficulties and acceptance of the ambivalences of life. For Oates, of course, problems of self-acceptance are basically of a religious character. And the forming of Christ in the personality is a Christian way of speaking of what I mean by self-transcendence.[34]

SELF-REALIZATION IN CONTEXT: REVISIONING PASTORAL COUNSELING

Despite the dominant influence of Rogers and the theme of self-realization after the war, Oates's cautious approach became more common among pastoral counselors by the end of the fifties as they found it more and more difficult to accept a simple equation between self-realization and the traditional Christian ideal of spiritual growth. As popular culture became more and more preoccupied with a narrow, private ideal of self-realization as the fulfillment of the self's every wish, pastoral theologians looked for a way to distinguish pastoral counseling that would at the same time set limits to self-realization.

The Contexts of Pastoral Counseling

The defining element that many theologians hit upon, led by a revisionist Seward Hiltner, was *context,* which Holifield gives a threefold specification.[35] From the *psychological* perspective, the context was the interpersonal relationship, of which Harry Stack Sullivan was a favorite theorist. The social self was regarded as perhaps the best way of setting limits to self-realization and correlating it with the traditional Christian ideal of spiritual growth. From the *theological* viewpoint, interpersonal psychology needed a larger context, and God was characterized as the ultimate context in which self-realization occurs. In this context of God's activity in the world, it was recognized that genuine self-realization required self-denial. And when, from a *practical* orientation, it was asked how these theological insights would actually affect counseling, the answer was in terms of the church as context, with its distinctive setting, expectations, relationships, and aims and limitations.

Clinebell's "Revised Model"

While the continuing work of Hiltner, Wise, Johnson, and Oates contributed significantly to the revisioning of pastoral counseling through the sixties, the dominant influence in the movement was Howard Clinebell's 1966 *Basic Types of Pastoral Counseling.*

Dissatisfied with the inadequacy of the prevailing Rogerian-psychoanalytic approach for pastoral counseling, Clinebell set out to provide a "revised model" of "relationship-centered counseling." Employing the contributions of family group therapy, role-relationship marriage counseling, transactional analysis, crisis intervention theory, reality therapy, existential psychotherapy, and ego psychology, Clinebell based his revised model "not on insight-oriented, uncovering psychotherapy, but on relational, supportive, ego-adaptive, reality-oriented approaches to therapy."[36]

In contrast to the prevailing model of the forties and fifties, Clinebell wanted to move: 1) from the formal, structured counseling interview as the dominant operational model, toward less formal and structured settings; 2) from the client-centered method as normative, toward appropriate sustaining, guiding, inspiring, confronting, teaching, and encouraging methods; 3) from insight as the central goal, toward enhancing a person's ability to relate in mutually need-satisfying ways; from the concepts of 4) unconscious motivation and 5) childhood roots of adult behavior, toward conscious material and contemporary relationships (focusing on the *between* rather than the *within*).[37]

But if Clinebell sought a significant shift in method to a more relationship-centered and action-oriented approach, his goal clearly remained that of self-realization. Agreeing with William Glasser that inability to fulfill essential personal needs is the basic problem brought to therapy, Clinebell combined Glasser's two essential needs (to love and be loved, and to feel worthwhile) into one: "to experience authentic love in a dependable relationship." Derived from this basic need are others: 1) a sense of worth, 2) responsible living, 3) inner freedom, 4) a sense of meaning, and 5) a loving, trustful relationship with God. Thus pastoral counseling helps "people handle their problems of living more adequately and grow toward fulfilling their potentialities...by helping them reduce the inner blocks which prevent them from relating in need-satisfying ways." By focusing on growth "toward the fulfillment of [one's] unique personhood," Clinebell clearly sees self-realization as the goal of counseling, but he includes in self-realization the development of more meaningful relationships with neighbor and God.[38]

Because he understands the church's purpose as the increase of the love of God and neighbor, Clinebell sees sound pastoral counseling, with its aim of helping us to love, as headed in the same direction as the church. Counseling can help us to overcome the alienation from ourselves, from others, and from God that is the essence of sin. Indeed, in Clinebell's view, the great theological issues—sin and salvation, guilt and forgiveness, judgment and grace, spiritual death and rebirth—are at the heart of counseling. "In a real sense *rebirth* to wider worlds of meaning and relationship is the ultimate goal of pastoral counseling."[39] Here we see a foreshadowing not only of our theme of self-transcendence (wider worlds of meaning and relationship), but also of those special instances of self-transcendence called conversions (rebirth). Before developing this theme of self-realization as self-transcendence and conversion, however, we must consider Clinebell's most recent version of the "revised model" in his 1984 *Basic Types of Pastoral Care and Counseling.*

The "Revised Model" Revised

Clinebell's personal and professional experience during the twenty years between the first and second editions of *Basic Types* brought about several important changes in his revision of the "revised model"—the new holistic liberation-growth model. The changes, however, are all incorporated into an approach that emphasizes two of the basic elements of the previous generation: 1) self-realization (growth) in 2) the context of the church's pastoral care. Among the many changes, I will focus here on those that relate to the meaning of self-realization.

For the new model the overarching goal of all pastoral care and counseling is to "liberate, empower, and nurture wholeness centered in Spirit." Because "spiritual and ethical wholeness is the heart of all human wholeness," they must be central concerns in pastoral care and counseling. Integrating both psychological and theological insight, pastoral care and counseling should be "holistic, seeking to enable healing and growth in all dimensions of human wholeness."[40]

Clinebell specifies six interdependent dimensions of personal life that must be included in growth toward wholeness at every stage of development.[41] 1) "Enlivening one's mind"–both left and right brains–"involves development of all our resources for thinking, feeling, experiencing, envisioning, and creating." 2) "Revitalizing one's body" means using, experiencing, and enjoying our bodies more effectively, fully, and lovingly. 3) "Renewing and enriching one's intimate relationships" is essential because our personalities are formed and transformed in such caring relationships. 4) "Deepening one's relationship with nature and the biosphere" requires increased ecological awareness, communion, and caring. 5) "Growth in relation to the significant institutions in one's life" demands involvement in the transformation of unjust social, political, and economic structures of violence, exploitation, and oppression. 6) "Deepening and vitalizing one's relationship with God" is the key to human flowering in all the other dimensions because coming alive in our relationship with God means coming alive at the center of our selves where all the dimensions of our being intersect and are unified. For Clinebell, spiritual wholeness means both that there is a spiritual dimension in all human problems and that basic spiritual needs are basic human needs.[42]

In specifying the various dimensions of wholeness in his liberation-growth model, and by emphasizing the unifying function of spiritual wholeness, Clinebell is clearly detailing the many areas in which we realize our selves through the single, though differentiated desire for self-transcendence. Just as clearly, he is explicitly including in his perspective not only the concerns of pastoral counseling but also those long dealt with in the Catholic tradition under the rubric of spiritual direction.

SELF-REALIZATION AS SELF-TRANSCENDENCE

While major modern authors on pastoral counseling like Hiltner, Wise, and Johnson have emphasized self-realization, they have also appreciated its ambiguity, and struggled with the issue of relating it to a traditional ideal of spiritual growth that includes the necessity of self-denial. Can psychological ideals of self-realization, self-fulfillment, and self-actualization be reconciled with traditional Christian ideals of self-denial, self-surrender, and self-sacrifice? Clinebell clearly opts for an affirmative answer in his holistic emphasis on growth, but assumes the possibility of reconciliation rather than providing a critical explanation of it.

Self-Realization and Self-Denial

If self-realization means self-fulfillment in the narcissistic sense of satisfying one's every wish, then it must be rejected as not only anti-Christian but antihuman. Such fulfillment is an impossible illusion. If self-denial means denial or sacrifice of the true self and its radical exigencies, then it must be rejected as not only antihuman but anti-Christian. Such denial would sacrifice the possibility of love. But we must affirm self-realization as the fulfillment of the exigencies of our true selves, just as we must affirm self-denial as the rejection of any interest, desire, or wish of the self that interferes with the realization of our true selves.

Self-Transcendence

Self-transcendence, incorporating both authentic self-realization and genuine self-denial, embodies the radical dynamism of the Christian spiritual life. Through self-transcendence the self is not sacrificed, but realized in its authentic being. But the realization of the true self in its drive for meaning, truth, value, and love rejects any self-centered striving for happiness through fulfillment, requiring that one empty oneself (even losing one's life) in the loving service of the neighbor. Self-transcendence, then, insists on the paradoxical view that authentic self-realization results not from an attempt to fulfill one's wishes, but from a movement beyond oneself in an effort to bring about the good of others. Here a brief summary of the dimensions of self-transcendence will suggest the fuller discussion to follow in Chapter 5.

Self-transcendence occurs in our effective response to the radical desire of the human spirit for meaning, truth, value, and love. This drive manifests itself in a series of interconnected questions. Our questions seek meaning in experience through understanding, but not just any meaning; through reflective questions we also seek evidence to establish truth in realistic judgments. And in practical matters, judgments lead to questions about value: what am I going to do? Finally, our decisions must be supported by the matrix of affectivity that surrounds and permeates the questioning process: to what shall I commit myself in love? Every achievement of creative understanding, realistic judgment, responsible decision, and generous love is an instance of self-transcendence. Such cognitive, moral, and affective self-transcendence to which the gospel calls us in service of the neighbor—and nothing less—is the criterion of authentic self-realization.

Conversion

While instances of self-transcendence occur in every life, the gospel calls us to *lives* of self-transcendence—thus the issue of conversion, of the transformation of our selves into dependable, life-giving springs of self-transcending discoveries, decisions, and deeds. Here I will anticipate a fuller discussion of conversion in Chapter 7 by briefly outlining four dimensions of Christian conversion—special instances of self-transcendence that transform our lives in fundamental ways.

In *moral* conversion we shift our criterion of decision from self-centered satisfaction to neighbor-oriented value. But we can meet this challenge to decide for value consistently only when we fall in love. Only through the *affective* conversion of our selves into beings-in-love can we escape our egocentric gravity and regularly decide to act in accord with our best judgments. But our best judgments may be bound to the conventional values of family, peers, or society. Only in *cognitive* conversion do we discover that the criterion of the true and the valuable is in our own self-transcending judgments and not somewhere "out there." Transcendence of socially and culturally limited values requires such critical appropriation of our own cognitive and moral powers. Still, even after years of seriously striving to live a life of value, one can ask: why be moral at all? As Job discovered, only the radical reorientation of life that allows God to move from the periphery to the center affords a lasting answer to this devastating question. Such a surrender of the illusion of absolute autonomy is possible only for the person who totally falls in love with a mysterious God. In this radical *religious* conversion, the self's autonomy is relativized and one's life is recognized as the gift it is. By liberating our capacities for self-transcendence in every dimension, pastoral counseling and spiritual direction enable us to respond to the gospel call to such radical conversion of life.

In the concept of self-transcendence, pastoral counselors and spiritual directors can integrate psychology and theology by seeing them as two complementary interpretations of the single radical desire of the human spirit. By reaching beyond ourselves through creative understanding, realistic judgment, responsible decision, and generous love, we both realize our authentic being (true self) and respond to the gospel's call to loving service of the neighbor. A psychology that understands self-realization as self-transcendence and a theology that recognizes the gospel as a call to self-transcendence require no reconciliation, only the discovery of their intrinsic unity as interpretations of the same fundamental human dynamism for self-transcendence.

But such discovery of self-transcendence as integrating psychological and theological perspectives for a unified pastoral counseling and spiritual direction requires that we understand exactly what we mean by "self," one of the most common, but slippery terms in both ordinary and technical language. This will be the task of the following chapter.

Chapter 3

Understanding the Self

We have tracked the changing ideals of the self through the history of the American pastoral counseling movement, but to this point we have not identified exactly what this self is that has so pre-occupied the pastoral counseling movement. For the most part, the authors presume various common-sense understandings of the self, and focus on the question of what stance to take toward it—denial, love, mastery, control, realization. The historical framework has given us some context for situating the different interpretations of Mary's development and conversion that we examined in Chapter 1, but terms like "self," "ego," and "person" still remain to be clarified. This chapter will consider these and other terms, like "subject," the "I," and the "me," in order to establish precisely what we mean by "self" when we speak not only of self-denial, self-realization, and self-transcendence, but also of the especially problematic "self-love."

Without a precise understanding of the self, the meaning of self-transcendence will remain vague, leaving pastoral counseling and spiritual direction without an integrated theoretical base, and pastoral counselors and spiritual directors without an effective practical appreciation of their clients' radical desires and possibilities. The dynamic understanding of the self we will work toward must be complex: multidimensional and interdisciplinary. Integrating insights from philosophy and theology as well as psychology, it will be defined in relation to, and include within it, basic meanings of difficult terms like person, ego, subject, the "I," the "me," identity, consciousness, the unconscious, character, conscience, and, of course, desire.

FROM PERSON TO SELF: A BRIEF HISTORY

While the meaning of the term "self" is too elusive to allow us to begin with a definition, we can start with a clue emerging from the close connection between self and interior subjectivity. In his *Confessions,* Augustine explicated his entry into himself in his search for a God who was more intimate to him than he was to himself. But it would be more than a millennium before interiority began to be plumbed again in a systematic way. Until the modern period the individual was dealt with less in the interior, subjective, first-person terms of "self" and more in the external, objective, third-person terms of "person." A grasp of the Christian tradition's meaning of person, therefore, is essential background for understanding the self that is central to pastoral counseling and spiritual direction.

The English word "person" reaches back to the Latin *persona* (*personare,* to sound through) and the Greek πρόσωπον (face, actor's mask). As a technical term it was first used in early Christian reflection on the Trinity and the Incarnation (Tertullian). Boethius provided the first philosophical definition: *"Persona est naturae rationalis individua substantia"* [A person is an individual substance of a rational nature]. With certain modifications this definition moved through medieval thinkers such as Thomas Aquinas, Richard of St. Victor, and Duns Scotus and into modern theological thought, as in Karl Rahner's encyclopedia *Sacramentum Mundi:* "The actual unique reality of a spiritual being, an undivided whole existing independently and not interchangeable with any other...belong[ing] to itself and...therefore its own end in itself...[with an] inviolable dignity."[1]

This basic meaning of "person" emerged from the interaction of Jewish and Christian religious experience with Greek philosophy. At the core of this religious experience is the person's free decision to respond to God's invitation to an intimate relationship. The Christian attempt to use Greek philosophical concepts such as "nature" and "substance" for its understanding and articulation of this experience gradually effected a transformation of these concepts. From a metaphysics of being, with its notion of the human individual as an infinite spirit trapped in a finite body, there developed a Christian theology of historical experience with its understanding of the person as an embodied spirit of absolute significance and destined for resurrection. In this sense, a person is an essentially social being, constituted precisely as person through its relationship with other free, independent, historical beings. A person is a concrete unity of individuality and universality, of immanence and transcendence; it subsists in itself, but is open to all reality. It is with this meaning of "person" that the Christian tradition has designated the absolute mystery that is God as "personal." Divine life is understood as the immanent perfection of God's being realized in a multiple personal act of knowing and loving. It is this personal God to whom Christians are related in faith. And it is in this sense of personal as relational that the tradition has understood women and men to be created in God's image and likeness. Indeed, it was the tradition's attempt to understand the human and divine dialectically in terms of each other that led to a meaning of person not only as independent and intellectual but also as relational and free in self-creative love.

Still, despite the significant development in the meaning of "person" from Greek philosophy to medieval Christian theology, the approach remained basically one of treating an essentially first-person, subjective reality in third-person, objective terms. It was not until the early modern period that the Augustinian theme of interiority was resumed in a significant way by philosophers like Descartes and religious thinkers like Pascal.

Descartes, though aware interiorly only of his thinking, assumed that it required a thinker, a self, which he understood as spiritual substance.[2] This thinking self became his first principle of philosophy. Pascal further identified the self with all striving, including feeling and willing as well as knowing. Locke pressed Descartes' doubt to include even the permanent, substantial nature of the self, which he understood to be the person as perceived by herself or himself: "I am a self only for myself and a person for others." The existence of the self, the seat of personal identity, requires continuing consciousness of oneself from past into present.[3] Hume also challenged the substantial nature of the self, finding it impossible to intuit a permanent self. Try as he might to catch himself independent of a particular perception of heat or cold, of pain or pleasure, he could never observe anything but the perception.

Further emphasis on subjectivity came from Kant, Hegel, and Kierkegaard. Kant distinguished between the phenomenal self, which, like other phenomena, can be known, and the noumenal self, which can only be inferred as a basic condition of knowing. Only in moral consciousness of freedom and duty does Kant's true ethical self know itself. For Hegel, the self was revealed through a process of differentiating self from non-self and discovering its presence in the non-self. Self-consciousness is reached only by the self externalizing or alienating itself. Kierkegaard also focused on alienation, but alienation of the self from God. The self constitutes itself by freely accepting its dependence on God; despair comes from estranging oneself from God. *Pugno, ergo sum* best suggests the reality of the self constituted through the will's struggle to reach the authentic, religious level of existence.

Later authors understood the self to have several aspects. William James understood the self as the sum of all that one knows oneself to be. Self-awareness is a stream, revealing two aspects: an "I," or experienced continuity, and a "me," which includes many selves rooted in bodily existence. G. H. Mead also understood the self as twofold: the selves of the "me," which result from social interaction, and the fictitious "I," which is always off-stage. Martin Buber saw the self constituted in the same dialogic way, but extended the dialogue to include nature and God. H. Richard Niebuhr rooted his theology of the responsible self in a similar triadic pattern of dialogue.

Mainstream empirical psychology did not follow James in his interest in the self. Existential-humanistic psychology has focused on the self, however; and certain psychoanalytic theorists have given major attention to the related concept of the ego and, more recently, even to the self. Existential-humanists such as Abraham Maslow, Carl Rogers, and Rollo May see the self as a set of radically human potentials that must be actualized, realized, or fulfilled through striving for an immanent ideal. Neo-Freudians like Karen Horney, Heinz Hartmann, and Erich Fromm helped move a more fully personal ego than Freud's to the center of the psychoanalytic stage. And Erik Erikson has not only traced the psychosocial development of ego-identity, but also distinguished and related the unconscious ego that integrates experience and the conscious "I," the live, numinous center of awareness. Psychoanalytic object-relations theorists and self psychologists such as D. W. Winnicott, Ronald Fairbairn, Otto Kernberg, and Heinz Kohut have focused on the development of the true self in the context of supportive interpersonal relationships, especially the relationship between infant and nurturing parent. Victor Frankl, an existentialist with a psychoanalytic background, centers on meaning as the constitutive reality of the self. In his view, self-actualization is not something that can be successfully sought after; self-actualization is only possible as a side-effect of striving for self-transcendence.

This reference to self-transcendence in Frankl's perspective signals the completion of our overview of the historical development from person to self and the transition of our considerations to a constructive theory of the self. As we move forward we will retain the notion of person along with that of self, of course, anticipating a comprehensive perspective in which the objective, third-person reality of an embodied, historical person will not be replaced but taken up and transformed by the subjective, first-person interiority of self. The same person who is observed at a distance is also a self who is immediately present to itself; "self" adds interiority to "person." The constructive phase begins with an attempt to clarify and situate a particularly difficult term, the "ego."

EGO: FROM CONSCIOUS TO UNCONSCIOUS

We begin our constructive reflections on the self with a consideration of the ego because of its importance, its difficulty, and its peculiar relation to self, person, and the "I." The term "ego" is important because of the major role it has played in many and very different modern philosophies and psychologies. It is difficult because it has represented, usually without warning, several different realities, both conscious and unconscious. Its relation to self, person, and the "I" is peculiar because it is a first-person word (like "I") used in a third-person manner (like "person") to represent a subjective reality (like "self"). If all this were not enough, "ego" is also a popular word in ordinary language, as in the expression, "He has a big ego." Sometimes "ego" seems to be equivalent to "self"; at other times, as in Jung's system, the two words definitely point to different realities. In any case, the two terms are so closely related that, if we can establish some clarity on what "ego" means, it should clear part of the conceptual deck for our attempt to construct a comprehensive understanding of the self.

Etymologically, of course, "ego" is simply the Latin word for "I." But that linguistic simplicity masks the term's complicated and confusing theoretical history. Although "I" is usually understood as having a first-person, experiential meaning, "ego" has often been used theoretically as having a third-person, hypothetical meaning. We can take two examples, one from philosophy and one from psychology.

We have already made reference to Kant's distinction between the phenomenal self and the noumenal self. One of the great philosophers directly influenced by Kant was the German Transcendental Idealist, J. G. Fichte. In order to prove that practical, moral reason is the absolute ground of all knowledge, Fichte postulated the ego as a supreme principle. From this sovereignly independent ego is deduced all other knowledge. This transcendental ego is neither self-evident nor even knowable, because it is not an object of knowledge but rather the condition of any knowledge. Notice that this ego is not an experienced "I,"but a postulated, hypothetical entity considered necessary for the existence of empirical self-consciousness. We shall leave this meaning of "ego" to the historians of philosophy.

Over a century later, from the entirely different perspective of psychoanalysis, Freud also postulated a hypothetical ego. Although he first used the term in the sense of the conscious "I" or self, Freud's truly distinctive meaning of "ego" is the hypothetical entity (or, more accurately, group of functions) he later postulated as the central player in his tripartite structural theory of the unconscious: id, ego, superego. Of the three, the ego may be closest to consciousness, but Erik Erikson, one of the most influential psychoanalytical theorists, has insisted on its intrinsically unconscious nature: "We become aware of its work but never of it."[4] Indeed, as an unconscious inner organizer of experience, the ego does for us what we could never consciously do for ourselves. Erikson explains: "Only after we have separated the 'I' and the selves from the ego can we consign to the ego...the domain of an inner 'agency' safeguarding our coherent existence by screening and synthesizing...all the impressions, emotions, memories, and impulses which try to enter our thoughts and demand our action, and which would tear us apart if unsorted and unmanaged by a slowly grown and reliably watchful screening system."[5]

While it is this meaning of "ego" as an inner organizer of experience that I will be carrying forward as we move on in this study, for the sake of clarity we should briefly contrast it to Jung's use of the term which we saw in Chapter 1. The contrast here is striking because Jung explicitly defines "ego" as the center of consciousness. Though this meaning of "ego" differs radically from Freud's, it is a particularly straightforward use of the word, equivalent to "I." Indeed, in another system Jung's "ego" might be named "self," but not so in Jung's, because in contrast to Jung's quite ordinary meaning of "ego" is his rather extraordinary definition of "self" (usually capitalized, "Self"). For Jung the Self is the subject of the total psyche, both conscious and unconscious. Postulated rather than experienced, the Self is Jung's entry in the hypothetical field, an ideal personality hinted at in the dream symbolism of a mandala. In contrast to Jung's Self as "transcendental postulate," "self" in this study will refer to a conscious, immediately experienced reality. And "ego," differing from both Fichte and Jung, will designate Freud's inner agency, the unconscious organizer of experience, a dimension of the total personal reality that, as conscious, is the self's "I." In short, from here on, I will use "ego" to mean the unconscious side of the self's "I."

Before moving ahead, we should pause briefly to consider one particularly significant interpretation of the ego as an unconscious, inner organizer of experience, an interpretation by Herbert Fingarette that will foreshadow and complement my understanding of the self in its radical desire for transcendence. Working from a psychoanalytic perspective, Fingarette understands the ego as a fundamental unifying drive toward meaning and integration. Distinct from the pleasure principle, this autonomous drive is what Freud called "the irresistible advance toward a unification of mental life." When the typical client comes to therapy because she or he is unhappy and finds no meaning in the unhappiness, the analyst addresses the lack of meaning as well as the unhappiness, lest the therapy result only in adjustment and not in personal integration.[6]

Given this view of ego as a unifying drive toward meaning, Fingarette is able to specify a structural meaning of anxiety as the breakdown of this drive. Ego is the drive toward integration, organization, meaning; anxiety is the failure of ego in this drive: disintegration, disorganization, meaninglessness. Anxiety is a uniquely provocative threat to ego, a threat that disrupts central ego integrity. Anxiety is ego-disorganization, ego-disintegration. Ego and anxiety are two sides of the same coin. When the drive for meaning functions properly, it is called "ego"; when it is threatened, we speak of anxiety. Anxiety in this structural sense sometimes produces the characteristic affect of anxiety-feelings. Following Karen Horney, Fingarette distinguishes two general kinds of anxiety: neurotic anxiety occurs when the ego falters in a normal environment; normal anxiety occurs when the ego fails in the face of universal human events—illness, catastrophe, death. Later we will see how the ego develops; but now we can note that the form of anxiety at any point in personal development is related to the kind of ego-integrity that is threatened—for example, separation-anxiety when the ego is primarily oriented to the relationship with the nurturing parent.[7]

Now that we have considered the unconscious, and postulated ego as a unifying drive for meaning, we will shift in the following sections to the conscious, experienced dimension of the self, the dialectic of the "I" and the "me." Before long we will be meeting the drive for meaning again as it emerges as a central dimension of the radical desire for self-transcendence within the conscious realm of the self.

THE CONSCIOUS "I": THE SELF-AS-SUBJECT

Having located the ego in the unconscious dimension of the self, we must turn our attention to its conscious partner, the subjective "I," and then to the "I's" objective alter, the "me." We must not expect an easy time of it, for over the centuries few philosophical or psychological concepts have proven as resistant to clarification. Nothing seems more familiar, more intimate than the "I," yet for philosophical and psychological inquiry nothing has been more elusive. The subjective "I" is always one step ahead of its pursuers, leaving only the objective "me" for the analyst's net. We can reflect on the "me," but the "I," precisely as subject, can only be experienced.

Despite the emphasis psychoanalyst Erik Erikson understandably gives to the unconscious ego, he insists just as firmly on the significance of the conscious "I": "One should be really decisive and say that the 'I' is all-conscious, and that we are truly conscious only insofar as we can say I and mean it." For Erikson, the "I" is "the ground for the simple verbal assurance that each person is a center of awareness in a universe of communicable experience, a center so numinous that it amounts to a sense of being alive, and more, of being the vital condition of existence."[8] On this sense of "I" Erikson refers us to William James, quoting a key passage from his *Psychology: The Briefer Course:*

> Whatever I may be thinking of, I am always at the same time more or less aware of *myself,* of my *personal existence.* At the same time it is *I* who am aware; so that the total self of me, being as it were duplex, partly known and partly knower, partly object and partly subject, must have two aspects discriminated in it, of which for shortness we may call one the *Me* and the other the *I.*[9]

William James's reflections on the duplex self are probably the single most influential source we have on the topic. As such, they are a key element in our attempt to clarify the reality of the self, and require serious attention. As James considered each aspect of the self, the "me" (as we shall see later) gave him no difficulty; but the "I" proved to be very tricky. A self-described radical empiricist, James was attempting to steer a clear course between the shallow waters of classical empiricism and the rocky cliffs of idealism. Wanting to take the "I" seriously as both continuous and experienced, he was willing neither to join Hume in dismissing the "I" because its permanence could not be intuited nor to postulate with Kant a nonexperienced transcendental "I." James's solution, rather, was in the conception of consciousness as a *stream,* with successive states or thoughts, each one distinct but taking up or appropriating the preceding one. There is no substantial identity of a metaphysical thinking "I," but a functional identity of successive states or thoughts—the thoughts themselves being the thinkers. "I" and "me" are names for what Thought is emphasizing at any point in the stream. The stream with its passing states of consciousness is all psychology needs; postulating the "I" as a substantial principle of unity is, as a possibly punning James says, "superfluous."[10] For James, explicitly restricting himself to a psychological perspective, distinct, successively appropriating Thoughts adequately explain the continuity of the "I" we experience.

James is satisfied, but some readers may be a bit suspicious of his capitalized Thoughts that are thinkers. Whether Thought is more radically empirical than the "I" may depend on our notion of "experience." In any case it is crucial that James does not end by affirming the "I" as a central personal reality more permanent than passing states—as, in our context, a radical principle of self-transcendence. Perhaps we should take a second look at the duplex self. James begins by distinguishing "whatever I may be thinking of" from the simultaneous reality of being "more or less aware of *myself, of my personal existence.*" This is a key distinction, but it is not clear exactly how James understands it. In the first instance there is clearly the presence of some *object* ("whatever") to a subject ("I"). But in the second it is not clear whether there is the presence of an object ("myself") to a subject ("I") or the presence of a *subject* ("I") to itself. Despite the important difference between "*thinking* of" and "*aware* of," James' language does not make clear which of two radically different kinds of psychic reality is at stake here.

The next sentence ("At the same time it is *I* who am aware...") suggests that James may have been thinking in both of the above instances of the same kind of presence, of the presence of an object to a subject. Otherwise, "*I* who am aware," which clearly seems to be a reference to subjective self-presence, would be redundant if "more or less aware of myself" in the first sentence referred to the presence of a subject to itself rather than of an object to a subject. To use an analogy that is at once grossly inadequate as well as anachronistic, James may have been thinking not of a TV set that is showing a picture and is simultaneously "on" (indeed, being "on" is a condition of showing a picture), but of a set that is showing a "picture within a picture" (two objects: "myself" more or less, within "whatever"). Of course, since being "on" is *not* being conscious, TV sets present pictures not to themselves but to us; my apologies!

Sufficiently confused? Well, hold on to your remote controls—it becomes even more interesting as James goes on to align "known," "object," and "me," and to group "knower," "subject," and "I" together. This may seem fine at first glance, but what are the implications? As an object, the "me" can presumably be known. But is it only objects that can be known? What about subjects? What about the "I"? Can the knowing "I" know itself *as a subject?* The way James arranges his line-up does not encourage us to think so.

In a recent book, Owen Flanagan, a contemporary follower of James, discusses the issue in terms of what he calls "self-consciousness."[11] He distinguishes self-consciousness in terms of two ends of a spectrum—as weak and strong, and as low-level and high-level. Strong (high-level) self-consciousness is definitely a matter of self-reflection, the self reflexively thinking about, knowing itself as an object. At the other end of the spectrum is weak (low-level) self-consciousness, which Flanagan identifies with James's reality of being "more or less aware of *myself....*" Here Flanagan says very little, and is no clearer than James. He wants to distinguish this awareness, this "sense that the experience is the subject's experience" from explicit self-representation, but he explains it as a different degree of self-consciousness, not a different kind of psychic presence.

Because a precise grasp of the nature of the conscious "I" is absolutely essential for understanding the self in its desire for transcendence, I will leave James for a few paragraphs now, and turn to a direct, straightforward consideration of the question. With the help of Bernard Lonergan's analysis, we will pay particular attention to: consciousness not as the perception of objects, but as subjective experience; reality as known not insofar as it is an object, but insofar as it is *in act;* and consciousness not just as cognitive, but also as constitutive.[12] In his view of the self, Lonergan follows the general lines of the distinction between "I" and "me" characteristic of modern philosophy and psychology. Within this interior duality, however, Lonergan introduces a distinctive understanding of the "I" that adequately complements the clarity philosophers and especially psychologists have given to the "me" as socially constructed. This meaning of "I" is rooted in an understanding of consciousness as the self's constitutive presence to itself.

In order to clarify his notion of conscious intentionality or intentional consciousness, Lonergan focuses on such distinctively personal activities as understanding, judging, and deciding—all operations that are essentially personal in the sense that whenever they are performed the self pre-reflectively is aware of, is present to, or experiences itself operating. Such operations not only intend objects, then, but also render the operating self conscious. Thus, by their intentionality essentially personal operations make objects present to the self, and in the *same act,* by their consciousness, they simultaneously make the operating (in act) person present to itself—make it an "I." A person may, for example, be most intensely conscious, present to self, while absorbed, or, as we sometimes say, even "lost," in a powerful film. Such experience seems paradoxical if we identify consciousness not with the subject's self-presence within intentional activity, but rather with reflexive knowing, which would provide a competing object of attention. "Losing" oneself in an enthralling film, however, is the opposite not of consciousness but of focusing on oneself. In both cases the self referred to (as "lost" and as focused on) is the self-as-object; the self-as-subject does the "losing" in the first case and the focusing in the second. By recognizing consciousness as the subjective presence of a person to herself in the very act of viewing, it becomes clear how she can be both fully conscious and fully engrossed in the film simultaneously. This is not the reflexive self-consciousness of introspection. Reflexive knowing is a second act that a film viewer may perform, when, after turning off the VCR, she perhaps thinks about her own life in light of the film. In this case, a person is simultaneously present to herself in two different ways: as a subject (an "I") by consciousness, and as an object (a "me") by the intentionality of the reflexive act. In direct knowing (of a film) the self is known once, as subject; in reflexive knowing the self is known twice, as subject and as object. This key distinction between consciousness and reflexive knowing bears repeating: in consciousness the "I" is present to itself as a subject within intentional operations; in reflexive knowing the "me" is present as an object to the "I," which is simultaneously present to itself as subject.[13]

Consciousness, according to Lonergan's distinctive theory, not only reveals the self-as-subject, but also *constitutes* it as such. Unlike external objects, the self-as-subject experienced in consciousness does not exist without consciousness (in a deep coma, for example).[14] The "I" who understands, judges, and decides is not only revealed to itself in consciousness as intelligent, reasonable, and responsible, but is capable of understanding, judging, and deciding only through consciousness. The self is brought into being as an "I" by the very consciousness that reveals it to itself. We must be very clear about this: *you* do not exist because I experience you, but *I* (not my body but I who am a subject) exist because I experience myself as a subject. In short, consciousness is not only cognitive, it is also constitutive of the knowing self-as-subject, of the "I" that is cognitively present to itself.

So, I hear you asking, what is the point of all this? Does it really make any difference how we understand the "I"? A full answer will have to emerge as we develop our understanding of the self in its radical desire for transcendence, but now we can briefly anticipate that development by emphasizing the "I" as the dynamic principle of transcendence. Later I will insist that significant transcendence requires a strong self; now I want to stress that the very possibility of transcendence requires a self that is capable of reaching beyond itself, and that central to such a self is not an inert, opaque metaphysical substance or a solipsistic self-as-object, but a dynamic "I," a conscious unity crowning a drive rooted in our genes and permeating our entire beings.

While James accounts for our sense of personal continuity by positing Thoughts, distinct, but successive appropriating states in a stream of consciousness, Lonergan highlights the constitutive consciousness of the self-as-subject (the "I") in contrast to the reflexive knowing of the self-as-object (the "me"). The key difference here is that James's account moves away from our experience of the "I" while Lonergan's account allows us to assess it by appealing back to the data of consciousness in a normal process of verification. Because we do not experience ourselves as a series of passing states, even appropriating ones, we have no evidence to affirm James's account. James is quite clear on this: "States of consciousness themselves are not verifiable facts."[15] On the other hand, the data of consciousness do support an affirmation of the unity of the "I," of ourselves as subjects.

In our conscious presence to ourselves we experientially know ourselves as subjects; the unity of this "I" that is given in consciousness is part of the data of consciousness. Here one's epistemology becomes crucial: Is reality known only insofar as it is an *object,* or is it known rather insofar as it is *in act?* Following Descartes' lead, philosophical positions that recognize only the objectified data of consciousness can acknowledge as real only the objectified "me," not the "I" that is never experienced as *object*. But acknowledgment of the subjective presence of the "I" to itself as experienced within intentional *acts* allows one to move in a process of critical introspective inquiry from these experiential data of consciousness through understanding to an affirmation of the "I" in the very act of experiencing, understanding, judging, and deciding. Like all affirmations, this reflexive affirmation is of an object, but an object that is a subject. Although our presence to ourselves as subjects can only be experienced, the subject we experience can be objectively affirmed through introspection.[16]

In contrast to a process that takes its start from data given in the self-presence of consciousness, James sees the alternatives as "direct introspective acquaintance with our thinking activity as such, with our consciousness as something inward…," on the one hand, and consciousness as "a *postulate* [rather] than a sensibly given fact" on the other.[17] Lonergan's position understands introspection as a process, not a direct acquaintance; and consciousness as a condition, not an object, of introspection. At the same time, it understands facts not as sensibly given but as issuing from correct judgments; and data of consciousness as significantly different from data of sense.

As affirmed in the data of consciousness, the "I" is empirical, not a metaphysical Self or transcendental Ego postulated inside the person. Just as the self is simply the person as *conscious,* the "I," as the subjective pole of the self, is the radical desire of the human being for meaning, integration, and self-transcendence come to the luminosity of consciousness (sometimes called "soul," sometimes "spirit"). Persons are present to themselves because that is the way the human organism naturally works; affirmation of the "I" does not add an internal super-person named the "I," it simply confirms the person as conscious (TV sets—here we go again—turn "on" because of the way they are "wired," not because there is a super-set inside).

What, again, is the point of all this? Though both James and Lonergan give prominence to the conscious "I," at the bottom line it is in the difference between the two *accounts* of consciousness that we find the possibility of *affirming* this dynamic "I," the living question that drives everything that is peculiarly personal. This dynamic

"I" is central to the Christian life; without its affirmation, the gospel call to the self-transcendence of truth and love is as meaningless as the wind howling across a barren desert. Absent a dynamic "I," there remains only a truncated and thus distorted self, a self capable of aspiring to nothing more than one form or another of shallow individualism, the perfect pawn to be manipulated in a consumer society.

But while the "I" is distinct from the "me" in the duplex self, it is never separate from it; the self is one. So it is to the "me," the objective correlative of the "I," that we must turn in the next section, where James again awaits us.

"ME": THE SELF-AS-OBJECT

Following William James, I have to this point characterized the self as "duplex." But perhaps "dipolar" is a more illuminating term. What I mean by this is that the self has two distinct but not separate poles: a subject-pole and an object-pole, an "I" and a "me." These poles exist in a dialectical relationship. To understand this elliptical self we must understand both poles, the "I" and the "me," in their mutually influencing relationship. We have considered the "I"; now we must turn our attention to the object-pole, the "me."

James, we recall, names the "me" the "self as known," because for him only the objective self is known. He points out that it is difficult to draw a line between what we call "me" and what we call "mine." "Our fame, our children, the work of our hands," he says, "may be as dear to us as our bodies are, and arouse the same feelings and the same acts of reprisal if attacked." And even our bodies, which many have disowned or been glad to escape—are they, he asks, "simply ours, or are they *us*?"[18] Despite fluctuations among what is me, and what is mine, and what has nothing to do with me,

> *In its widest possible sense...a man's Me is the sum total of all that he CAN call his,* not only his body and his psychic powers, but his clothes and his house, his wife and children, his ancestors and friends, his reputation and works, his lands and horses, and yacht and bank-account. All these give him the same emotions. If they wax and prosper, he feels triumphant; if they dwindle and... die away, he feels cast down—not neces-

sarily in the same degree for each thing, but in much the same way for all.[19]

James considers three dimensions of this "me": the material "me," the social "me," and the spiritual "me."

The body is the most inner part of the *material "me,"* some parts of it more than others. Then come our clothes, which most of us identify with. Next come our families and our homes. "All these different things are the objects of instinctive preferences coupled with the most important practical interests of life. We all have a blind impulse to watch over our body, to deck it with clothing of ornamental sort, to cherish parents, wife, and babes, and to find for ourselves a house of our own which we may live in and 'improve.'"[20] And like our homes, also the things we collect, and especially those we make, become part of ourselves.

The *social "me"* consists in the recognition we get from those who matter to us. So we have as many social selves as there are persons or groups who recognize us and have an opinion of us we care about. Damage to these opinions is damage to self. We usually present a different "me" to each of those persons or groups. This is authentic enough in the case of a mother who shows one self to her young children and another to clients in her law practice. But we think differently about a politician who has a different self for every set of constituents. And what do we think of the teacher who has one self for administrators, another for faculty colleagues, another for students, another for secretarial staff, and still another for maintenance staff? For the man who falls in love, says James, the social self is susceptible to the heights of elation and the depths of dejection. "To his own consciousness he is not, so long as this particular social self fails to get recognition, and when it is recognized his contentment passes all bounds."[21]

By the *spiritual "me"* James means no one of the passing states of consciousness in particular, but rather the entire collection of these states of consciousness, the "psychic faculties and dispositions taken concretely," all of which can become an object of thought and awaken emotions.

> When we *think of ourselves as thinkers,* all the other ingredients
> of our Me seem relatively external possessions. Even within
> the spiritual Me some ingredients seem more external than

others. Our capacities for sensation, for example, are less intimate possessions, so to speak, than our emotions and desires;
our intellectual processes are less intimate than our volitional
decisions. The more *active-feeling* states of consciousness are
thus the more central portions of the spiritual Me. The very
core and nucleus of our self, as we know it, the very sanctuary
of our life, is the sense of activity which certain inner states
possess....It is as if they *went out to meet* all the other elements
of our experience.[22]

Having laid out the three basic constituents of the self's "me,"
James discusses feelings of the self (self-appreciation) and self-
seeking. Self-appreciation includes both self-complacency (self-
esteem, but also pride, conceit, vanity, arrogance) and
self-dissatisfaction (confusion, shame, mortification, but also
despair). "Like fear and like anger,...these opposite feelings of Self
may be aroused with no adequate exciting cause. And in fact we
ourselves know how the barometer of our self-esteem and confidence rises and falls from one day to another through causes that
seem to be visceral and organic rather than rational, and which certainly answer to no corresponding variations in the esteem in
which we are held by our friends."[23]

Under self-seeking James distinguishes bodily self-seeking
(actually, the material "me" in the widest sense), social self-seeking,
and spiritual self-seeking. Of these, social self-seeking (our desire
to attract admiration, our love of influence and power, and so
forth) is particularly important insofar as much of material-bodily
self-seeking (beautiful physique, stylish clothes, possessions) is
aimed at social ends, and much of spiritual self-seeking (at least in
the narrow, religious sense) is aimed at an exalted kind of social
good—the fellowship of saints, the presence of God.

While we all experience conflict and rivalry among these selves,
James suggests that common opinion orders them hierarchically,
"with the bodily me at the bottom, the spiritual me at the top, and
the extra-corporeal material selves and the various social selves
between."[24] And in each kind of "me" we distinguish between the
immediate, actual, and narrower and the remote, potential, and
wider, approving the latter in cases of conflict. James finds the
potential social "me" especially interesting when for reasons of
conscience we bear the loss of an actual self (condemnation by

family, friends, and so on) in pursuit of an ideal social self (approved by a higher—or highest possible—judge).[25]

Having outlined James' discussion of the "me"—the material, social, and spiritual selves—I must clarify the exact nature of the reality at issue here. It is crucial to recognize that *as known* the "me" in all its dimensions is a *psychic* reality. The material "me" is not simply one's physical body and clothes; not one's family and friends; not one's house and possessions. Rather, it is one's *perception* of these things, which may, of course, be quite different from the external reality, despite the power of that reality in shaping the "me." One's perception of oneself will not necessarily be more accurate than one's perception of another, and it will almost certainly be more emotionally charged. A teenage boy's sense of self can be crushed and distorted by an extreme acne condition. But a young woman may be 100 pounds at 5′8″, and still see herself as grossly overweight. The social "me" is not simply the recognition one gets, but one's perception of that recognition. The encouragement of one teacher can make all the difference in the world to a seventh-grader—it can, indeed, *make* her world. But another student who gets the same attention cannot believe that anyone could care about him. The spiritual "me" is not simply one's mind and heart, but one's perception of them. The discovery of one's musical or artistic talent can definitely shape a person's life. But in others real talent lies undiscovered and undeveloped, and, of course, the same is true for the whole range of spiritual potential. If a man thinks that religion is for women, his faith life—what we might call his religious "me"—suffers.

The fact that James discusses the psychic reality of the self's "me" in terms of material, social, and spiritual selves may support our naive inclination not only to reify the self, but also to then conceive of this "thing" we call the "me" as divided into "sub-things." We must continually remind ourselves that "self" means not some*thing* added to the person, but the subjective experience of the person as conscious. The self is real, but not a thing.[26] James's discussion of the material, social, and spiritual selves can most accurately be understood as a specification of various dimensions or aspects of the single "me," the self-as-object (which, itself, is only distinct, not separate, from the self-as-subject).

As a psychic reality, the "me" is a historical product of personal, especially interpersonal, experience. In the language of "self-cre-ation," we may say that if the self is constituted by consciousness, it is constituted as *this* self only through the concrete specifics of its own personal history, an experiential history of meaning and value. Indeed, as historically conscious modern philosophy has taught us, who we are as particular individuals is determined through time — not only by our particular experience of the present, but also by our particular memory of the past (whether or not it actually happened that way) and by our particular anticipation of the future (whether or not it actually turns out that way). As the self discovers and con-structs a world of meaning, it also constitutes itself in some specific concrete shape, gives itself a certain character. In other words, the "me," the self-as-object, is gradually created as this particular self through personal experience—discoveries, decisions, and deeds. This ongoing, historical constitution of the self-as-object through meaning and value occurs because its dialectical counter-pole, the "I," the center of conscious subjectivity, is a radical, self-creating drive for integrated meaning and value in self-transcendence.

We should recapitulate at this point. The self is the person pre-cisely as conscious—a dynamic, dipolar, dialectical, embodied, first-person reality constituted by consciousness and experienced as "I" (self-as-subject striving for meaning and value in self-transcending relationships) and "me" (self-as-object consisting of material, social, and spiritual selves). The ego is the unconscious correlative of the self's "I," a unifying drive toward integration, organization, and meaning.

Chapter 4

The Self in Post-Freudian Psychoanalytic Theory

Now that we have considered the dynamic, dipolar self, and distinguished the dialectical subject ("I") and object ("me") poles within this embodied, "first-person" reality of the conscious person, we are in a position to relate it to some important post-Freudian psychoanalytic conceptions of the self. The intention here is to be brief and suggestive rather than comprehensive and exhaustive. After background remarks about Freud, Heinz Hartmann, and C. G. Jung, we will consider transitional figures such as Melanie Klein, Harry Stack Sullivan, and Karen Horney, then such object-relations theorists as Ronald Fairbairn, D. W. Winnicott, Edith Jacobson, and Otto Kernberg, the linking developmental perspective of Margaret Mahler, and self psychologists like Heinz Kohut, George Klein, and James Masterson. We will conclude with integrative figures like Harry Guntrip and Erik Erikson.

BACKGROUND AND TRANSITION

Although Freud made attempts to move away from the classic scientific model of biological instincts to a more ego-oriented approach, the ego that became more and more central to his thought was the unconscious system-ego of his tripartite structural theory. He always took the conscious self for granted, and left it mostly implicit.[1] Heinz Hartmann later brought the ego to fuller conceptual clarity, as he turned it to the external world and endowed it with autonomy from both the id and the environment. But he, too, focused on the ego as part of a structural system, not on the ego as self.[2] C. G. Jung, as we have seen, went in a different direction on the ego/self question, but while his ego was more person-centered, his Self was a postulated ideal to be realized through a process of individuation.[3]

Melanie Klein did not focus on the self, but by concentrating on the internalization of significant interpersonal relations she was able to make a breakthrough to the psychic world of ego-object relations which Freud approached with the Oedipus Complex but was never able to fully exploit.[4] Harry Stack Sullivan also highlighted interpersonal relations and "self" language, but his self was more systemic than personal, and his "relations" were not with Klein's distinctive internalized objects, which later characterized the specifically object-relations approach. His view of the self as made up of reflected appraisals does however echo James's social "me."[5]

Karen Horney anticipated some of the later psychoanalytic focus on the self, distinguishing actual, real, and idealized selves. While for Horney the actual self is a person's total experience, the real self is an individual's unique sense of integration or wholeness, a deep source of growth. In contrast, the idealized self is a neurotic attempt to avoid conflict through self-glorification.[6]

OBJECT-RELATIONS THEORY

In Ronald Fairbairn we finally get a psychoanalytic theorist who both broke away from the grip of Freudian instinct theory and the structural ego, and moved explicitly into the world of object-relations. In contrast to the structural ego, Fairbairn proposed a personal ego, a subjective sense of "I." From birth the infant is a pristine, dynamic, and object-related whole ego. Inherent in this ego is an object-seeking life-drive: "libido is not primarily pleasure-seeking, but object-seeking."[7] From this originally whole ego evolve ego substructures by a process of splitting and introjecting bad and good objects in reaction to unhappy parental experience: libidinal ego and exciting object; antilibidinal ego and rejecting object; and central ego and idealized object. Fairbairn was particularly interested in the schizoid personality, which results from a combination of inner ego splitting and withdrawal from object relations. Fairbairn uses the language of "ego," but defines it in a personal way that moves in the direction of this study's "self," with which it is compatible though not equivalent (as is his object-seeking life-drive with the radical desire for self-transcendence).

D. W. Winnicott explicitly placed the self at the center of his perspective. For him, like Fairbairn, the infant is characterized by wholeness from the beginning. But rather than a process of splitting an ego given at birth, Winnicott saw a process of the emergence of a self that is merely potential in the newborn. Whether a true or false self emerges depends on the quality of the mother's responsiveness to the infant's object-relation needs. The facilitating environment of a "good enough" mother supports development of the infant's true self within meaningful relationships. Such basic ego-relatedness provides a life-long foundation for the self. Without such a supportive environment, the lively creativity of the true self is unrealized, and a false self develops in either rebellious reaction or meek conformity to this inadequate environment. "True" and "false" here signify not two selves, but two different shapes that the self may take in its development. In either case, I suggest that we can understand's Winnicott's "self" as a way of qualifying the concrete character the self-as-object (the "me") assumes through its earliest personal interactions.[8] Regarding Mary, this approach would focus on the unhappy relationship with her mother that goes back as far as she can remember.

Though originally working in the context of Hartmann's ego psychology, Edith Jacobson created a developmental understanding of the self along lines very similar to the views of Fairbairn and Winnicott. Jacobson took the notion of self ("one's own person") that Hartmann had distinguished from the ego,[9] and explicated its development in terms of object-relations. Out of a process of subject-object differentiation develop libidinal and aggressive drives in reaction to external objects perceived as good and bad. For Jacobson, libido is the essential drive of the self to live by relating to objects in the external world.[10]

Much of Jacobson's contribution, as well as Hartmann's and Fairbairn's, was brought together in the work of Otto Kernberg, who was strongly influenced by factors like self-object differentiation

and the internalization of the good and bad mother. Kernberg
viewed the psyche as structured by groups of internalized object-
relations: object images and self images, as well as their affects.[11]

Before moving from object-relations theorists to self psychologists, we should pause to consider the work of Margaret Mahler,
whose view of early development in terms of self-object differentiation relates to both groups of analysts. Mahler traced the infant's
development from non-differentiated states of autism and symbiosis to what she calls the infant's psychological birth in a process of
separation-individuation. After the first month of normal autism,
when the infant is essentially isolated from external stimuli, there
follows a period of symbiosis in which the infant is in a state of
fusion with its mother, a stage in which "I" and "not I" have not yet
been differentiated. After a few months the four-phase process of
separation-individuation begins: differentiation, practicing, rap-
prochement, and consolidation of individuality. Over the course of
a few years this maturational process—always deeply influenced by
interaction with parents—results in a subjective sense of bodily and
psychological identity and autonomous functioning. Although this
process features a struggle between a longing for independence
and a desire for attachment (reflecting my basic thesis on the self),
Mahler maintained that a strong early attachment between the
infant and mother supported autonomous exploration. We shall
see more of this interesting relationship between these two basic
desires in our later consideration of development.[12]

The infant's sense of self has recently been featured in the
developmental-psychoanalytical work of Daniel Stern, who explicitly departs from Mahler's basic view on separation-individuation.
In his assertion that infants experience a sense of an emergent self
from birth, Stern rejects an initial confusion of self and other, a sym-
biotic phase, and a period primarily devoted to the task of independence. In the first two years he sees emergent, core, subjective, and
verbal selves (each incorporating the previous, though all remaining
distinct), with the second year devoted as much to the creation of
intersubjective union with others as to the task of independence.[13]
During the first two months there is the *emergent* self which con-
structs a world of "otherness." In the next few months there is the
core self, the infant's experience of being an integral body. Then, in
the second half of the infant's first year, there arises the *subjective*

self, an awareness of emotion, and a concern to attune feelings to those of others. Finally, early in the second year there arrives, with the emergence of language and the birth of symbolization, the *verbal* self, vulnerable to alienation and the experience of shame and doubt, with resulting defense mechanisms and "false self." For the purposes of the present study, the differences between Mahler and Stern are not as important as the fact that both assert the existence of a self in relation to others by the end of the second year.

SELF PSYCHOLOGY

Heinz Kohut took a different angle on the self by understanding it as the structure of narcissism rather than its object. In Kohut's view, primary narcissism develops independently from the id, ego, and superego. Imperfect parental empathy leads it to differentiate into the grandiose self and the idealized parental imago. The former can develop into mature confidence and self-esteem, but its arrest can result in exhibitionism and grandiosity; the latter can integrate with the values of the ideal ego, but it can also de-rail into depression and fragmentation. Kohut echoes Winnicott's "good enough mother" in his view that the individual, from infancy on, needs the warm acceptance and loving support of empathic interaction that provides a sense of worthwhileness. Unfulfilled, this need leads to the aberrant self-development just mentioned: the pathological structuring of the self-as-object.[14]

Though not a follower of Kohut, George Klein also attempted to develop a psychoanalytic psychology of the self. Working within a more traditional Freudian framework than either Kohut or Fairbairn, Klein still managed to produce a view centered on the maintenance of self-integrity very similar to theirs. For him the need for a unified self is the fundamental motive underlying all else. Life is essentially a matter of struggling toward the resolution of incompatible aims in the context of this basic need for self-integrity. As a result, repression, anxiety, and other Freudian staples all get re-defined in relation to the self. Ego and id, for example, refer to what is and what is not owned by the self. Sexual activity is not for discharge of energy but for the self-value symbolized in sexual accomplishment. For the integrative purposes of our study, it is

important to note that Klein works out his focus on the resolution
of incompatible intrapsychic aims in relation to self-integrity
within the context of object-relations, thus bringing traditional
Freudian issues together with the two most important aspects of
contemporary theory—object-relations and the self.[15]

James Masterson sought a complete theory of the self that would
include both the intrapsychic Freudian structures and the creative
dimension of subjective experience. He called this the *real* self. This
real self, mostly conscious, is made up of "the intrapsychic images
of the self and of significant others, as well as the feelings associated
with these images, along with the capacities for action in the environment guided by those images."[16] The real self derives its images
mostly from reality, and aims at the adaptive mastery of reality. In
contrast, the false self is derived mostly from infantile fantasies, and
is directed toward the defensive avoidance of painful feelings. In
Masterson's view, the real self interrelates all its self-images (conscious or unconscious, realistic or distorted), including body
images, and recognizes within them a single, unique individual.
Masterson understands this real self as developing along the lines
we have seen in Mahler's view. His real self has similarities with the
understanding of self I am proposing in this study—for example, in
distinguishing self and ego and maintaining both, and in following
Erikson's view of the automatic, regulatory role of the unconscious
ego. There are also significant differences, however, between my
interpretation of the self and Masterson's; for example, Masterson
sees the ego as the "executive arm" of the self,[17] which seems to
bring it to the center of consciousness in a way I would not.

Masterson discusses ten capacities that characterize the real
self.[18] Even a summary list of these characteristics suggests what he
means by the real self: 1) the ability to experience deeply a wide
range of feelings; 2) the expectation of mastery and pleasure in life
as an entitlement; 3) the capacity for self-activation and assertion;
4) self-esteem; 5) the ability to soothe painful feelings; 6) the ability
to make and keep commitments; 7) creativity in problem-solving
and life patterns; 8) the capacity for intimacy; 9) the ability to be
alone without feeling abandoned; and 10) the capacity to recognize
continuity and sameness of self through time and space. In contrast to the healthy development (Mahler's separation-individuation) that leads to this real self, there is the abandonment

depression in the first three years that leads to a false self (the deflated false self of the borderline personality or the inflated false self of the narcissistic personality).

INTEGRATION AND IDENTITY

Few psychoanalytic theorists have focused on the self as explicitly and forcefully as Harry Guntrip. Influenced by Fairbairn and Winnicott, Guntrip stressed the psychodynamic, personal, and object-relational dimensions in Freud, over the scientific, physiological, and mechanistic. He viewed the newborn as a whole psyche with innate potential for developing into a true self within the supportive object-relationships that give meaning to our lives. Without such relationships, especially with the first care-giver, the true self is left unevoked, and false selves substitute for it. For Guntrip, psychoanalysis is a theory not just of the unconscious, but of the whole person, including the body, developing within more or less healthy object-relations. He rejects the id and its instinctual drives, and argues for one basic psychophysiological life-drive toward the world of objects, a drive that generates aggression when opposed. The self is the psychic dimension of the whole psychosomatic person energized by this drive. The self develops characteristics and a structural identity as it relates libidinally to the object-world.[19] Clearly, with Guntrip we have a psychoanalytic view of the self that is very compatible with my dynamic, dipolar interpretation.

The above reference to "identity" can be our cue to turn to that more widely known psychoanalytic theorist, Erik Erikson, whom we have already seen stressing the unconscious character of the ego, as well as the conscious nature of the "I." Erikson has often been grouped with the psychoanalytic theorists known as ego psychologists, such as Hartmann, but his work is really too creatively independent to be put in any school. One of the most original of Freud's followers, he was also particularly reluctant to explicitly break from the master on central points of doctrine. Thus, for example, while he reinterpreted the instinctual drives, he did not reject the id, as other contemporary theorists like Guntrip did. Erikson is not usually grouped with object-relations theorists, but few writers have so forcefully shifted the psychoanalytic center of gravity from intrapsychic conflict to interpersonal relations. Likewise, Erikson is not a self psychologist, but by his focus on identity he has done more than most theorists to bring the self to center stage.

Identity is usually associated with the adolescent "identity crisis" in discussions about Erikson's work, but it is so central a concept in his thought that it runs at various levels through the whole of the life cycle. Indeed, such is the centrality of Erikson's psychosocial identity that it integrates not only the "psycho" and the "social," but the past and the future, the conscious and the unconscious. Identity is "at once subjective and objective, individual and social," says Erikson.[20]

Identity involves a subjective sense of sameness and continuity as an active, alive individual, a sense that is sometimes intense, even exuberant. William James illustrates this in an 1878 letter to his wife: "I have often thought that the best way to define a man's character would be to seek out the particular mental or moral attitude in which, when it came upon him, he felt himself most deeply and intensely active and alive. At such moments there is a voice inside which speaks and says: 'This is the real me!'"[21] On the social side, identity "presupposes a community of people whose traditional values become significant to the growing person even as his growth assumes relevance for them."[22]

Although Erikson often writes, especially in his early works, of *ego* identity, he also makes it clear that identity is a quality of the whole person: "at one time...it will appear to refer to a conscious sense of individual identity; at another to an unconscious striving for a continuity of personal character; at a third, as a criterion for the silent doings of ego synthesis; and finally as a maintenance for an inner solidarity with a group's ideals and identity."[23]

As a response to the crisis of adolescence, Erikson stresses that the "integration of an identity is more than the sum of childhood identifications."[24] As "more," the identity that is an accomplishment of the young adult results from a *creative* act of self-understanding: "It is the accrued experience of the ego's ability to integrate all identifications with the vicissitudes of the libido, with the aptitudes developed out of endowment, and with the opportunities offered in social roles."[25] The creation of such an identity, building on but going beyond everything that came before, is clearly a major act of self-transcendence.

I must repeat here the epistemological caution about reification mentioned at the end of the previous chapter. Constant discussion about true self, false self, real self, idealized self, grandiose self, and even identity can seduce us into thinking about them as substantial entities, as things. They may be real, but they are no more things than the self is a thing. Like Freud's id, ego, and superego, these contemporary psychoanalytic selves must be understood as patterns or functions of psychic processes within the conscious person, not as entities added to the person.

The many views we have discussed here are by no means all compatible with each other. But as we moved away from Freud and Hartmann toward the theorists of object-relations and the self, a dominant pattern of development began to emerge. And it is the theme of this pattern, rather than the many variations, that I want to highlight for the purposes of the present study. Articulated in greatest detail by Mahler, this pattern is reflected in various ways in the work of the many different theorists reviewed, from Fairbairn and Winnicott to Masterson and Guntrip. This pattern of development proceeds from total undifferentiation and dependence to significant differentiation between self and other (and thus between subject and object poles) and independence of the self.

Although these psychoanalytic theorists mainly address the self that we have specified here as the self-as-object (the "me"), it is clear that Masterson, Erikson and Guntrip, especially, strain toward the integrity of the whole person and the subjective experience of the "I." But in every case we see possibilities of the self-as-object being structured in authentic or unauthentic patterns. And because the subject and object poles of the self can be distinguished but never separated, the "I" experiences itself in these patterns. But because the "I," the self-as-subject, is never completely identified with the "me," the self-as-object, the possibility of change, of transformation, of conversion always exists in the radical desire for self-transcendence. Whether realized in the formal setting of therapy or the spontaneous cauldron of daily life, this drive for the real, this creative desire for authentic interpersonal relations means that an individual is never finally condemned to today's false self. Though concretely rooted in an individual's personal history, the self-creating desire for meaning and value is in principle infinitely open to reality.

THE UNITY OF THE SELF

We have seen object-relations theorists like Fairbairn, Winnicott, and Guntrip stress the wholeness of the person. Fairbairn, for example, insisted on viewing the infant as a whole psychic self from the very beginning of life: "The pristine personality of the child consists of a unitary dynamic ego."[26] And Guntrip was just as adamant in his view of the psychosomatically whole person.[27] Though generally in agreement with Erikson, Guntrip took strong exception to Erikson's view of the human as made up of evolutionary layers in which the primitive past survives to wreak havoc in the present. Discussing the id and the ego, Erikson wrote that "the name 'id'...designates the assumption that the ego finds itself attached to this impersonal, this bestial layer like the centaur to his equestrian underpinnings: only that the ego considers such a combination a danger...."[28] Guntrip vehemently rejected the ineradicable dualism of the centaur's two hostile layers as undermining the goal of a mature, whole human person. He preferred Harry Stack Sullivan's view of the body as the biological substrate that is taken up into the personal self.[29]

This issue of the wholeness or unity of the person has been dealt with most comprehensively, perhaps, by Michael Polanyi and Bernard Lonergan. Both view the person as a multileveled reality, with each higher level integrating the lower levels into a greater unity.

Working from his distinction between subsidiary and focal awareness in personal knowing, Michael Polanyi specifies two distinct levels in knowledge and in reality, "that of a comprehensive entity and that of its particulars...." Then, starting with two comparatively low levels, a machine and its parts, Polanyi erects "a consecutively rising set of levels, right up to that of responsible human personhood." In his view, higher levels are dependent on lower levels, and although lower levels cannot account for successful higher level operations, inadequacies on lower levels—poor physical health, for example—can account for higher level errors or malfunctions. Also, within this scheme of levels, Polanyi sees desires of the body in conflict with the desire for truth or other goods of intrinsic excellence. Thus, the desire for truth becomes an act of self-compulsion, in which "the utmost straining of every clue pointing towards the true solution finally imposes a particular choice upon the chooser," who submits to a personal sense of responsibility. Though dependent on lower levels, the highest level introduces an integrating order of personal unity.[30]

For Bernard Lonergan, the person is explicitly a unity-in-tension. At any point in development a person is an individual, existing unity, differentiated physically, chemically, organically, psychically, and intellectually. Each level takes up or sublates the lower level into a higher integration. Personal development follows a law of limitation and transcendence, a law of tension. "On the one hand, development is in the subject and of the subject; on the other hand, it is from the subject as he is and towards the subject as he is to be." Thus development occurs only when the dynamism for change breaks through the inertia of the subject's existing stage. In personal change, of course, the tension is conscious. Anticipating the future can be terrifying. And when the development involved is intellectual, there is the deeper challenge of giving the pure desire to know its head, of allowing it to dominate one's knowing and living. "For the self, as perceiving and feeling, as enjoying and suffering, functions as an animal in an environment, as a self-attached and self-interested centre within its own narrow world of stimuli and responses. But the same self, as inquiring and reflecting, as conceiving intelligently and judging reasonably, is carried by its own higher spontaneity to quite a different mode of operation with the opposite attitudes of detachment and disinterestedness."[31]

So, for Lonergan, the tension of human consciousness consists in the fact of an ineluctable "opposition between a centre in the world of sense operating self-centredly and, on the other hand, an entry into an intelligently ordered universe of being to which one can belong and in which one can function only through detachment and disinterestedness." Thus in personal development the point of departure that is to be changed is "permanent in the self-centred sensitive psyche content to orientate itself within its visible and palpable environment and to deal with it successfully." And Lonergan makes it clear that the pure desire and the sensitive psyche are not "two things, one of them 'I' and the other 'It'. They are the unfolding on different levels of a single, individual unity, identity, whole. Both are I and neither is merely It." If our intelligence and reasonableness seem more us than our sensitive spontaneity, it is because of the higher integration the former succeed in imposing on the latter. But regardless of how successful the higher integration of intelligence and reasonableness is, Lonergan maintains that "the basic situation within the self is unchanged, for the perfection of the higher integration does not eliminate the integrated or modify the essential opposition between self-centredness and detachment. The same 'I' on different and related levels of operation retains the opposed characters."[32]

Such, as Lonergan sees it, is the unity of the person. The person is a unity, but a unity-in-tension. The person is a unity because its several levels are related through sublation, each higher level taking up and integrating the lower. But it is a unity-in-tension because even full integration does not eliminate the opposition between limitation and transcendence, between the self-centeredness of the sensitive psyche and the detachment and disinterestedness of the pure desire.

This permanent opposition may sound pessimistic to Guntrip, who stressed unity in contrast to the tension in what he regarded as Erikson's dualism. But, like it or not, such tension is the basic stuff of pastoral counseling and spiritual direction. For these ministries work toward realizing genuineness by lifting that tension into consciousness, which is, in Lonergan's view, "the necessary condition of the harmonious co-operation of the conscious and unconscious components of development."[33]

Now that we have considered the unity of the person, we can return to the related question of the unity of the self raised earlier, especially in connection with the bodily "me." For both Polanyi and Lonergan the highest level of the person is conscious, even though they consider it here in the third person, objective terms of person rather than in the first person, subjective terms of self. Lonergan does use the language of self, however, and we have already seen that he affirms the unity of the conscious "I."

The fact that we can affirm the unity of the "I" does not mean that it is a simple unity. The complex, multileveled character of our being introduces ambiguity into the conscious person's experience of self. Indeed, we experience that ambiguity every day. It is particularly clear in the relation between the "I" and the body. What are we to make of James's statement that "the *body* is the innermost part of the material me in each of us..."?[34] Are our bodies, as James puts it, *ours,* or are our bodies *us?* For example, we say things like "I feel great today," identifying with our bodies; we also say "This sprained ankle is killing me," distinguishing a body part from the self and even casting it against the self. *Are* we bodies, or do we *have* bodies? Certainly, we experience ourselves as embodied, but we usually do not say "I am a body." But we do say "I am..." fat or thin, tall or short, strong or weak, and so forth—using the same terms we use to characterize our bodies.

Again, I say that *I* play tennis, not that my body or my arms and legs play tennis. At the same time, I say that I *have* arms and legs, not that I am arms and legs. I can even imagine myself losing my arms and legs without losing my sense of "I," of who I am. I would be changed, but still the same "I." It is more difficult for me to imagine not being a tennis player, but that is possible, too. Of course, there is a huge difference between never having been a tennis player and being a former player. This ambiguity between the self's sense of "I" and body, rooted in the multileveled structure of the person, becomes conscious because of our ability to reflect back on the self. To put the point in Polanyi's terms, we can focus our knowing *reflexively* on our body (or on its particular parts) as well as simply *dwell* in the body as we focus on other things (which we usually do). When we dwell in our bodies, we identify with them: *I* play tennis. In fact, reflexive analysis of body parts in play can destroy the playing—paralysis through analysis! In this case, we are focusing on ourselves instead of on the ball. In tennis, as in other sports, we practice strokes and other moves endlessly so that we can make them our own or dwell in them, which frees us to focus exclusively on the ball and the game's action without thinking about or focusing on how we are playing. Athletes refer to high level indwelling as being in "the zone" (Maslow's "peak experience"): heightened subjectivity (presence to oneself as subject) within simultaneous intense attention to the action (focus on an object). So, we can ask the question again, *are* we bodies, or do we *have* bodies, and now give the odd answer, yes: we *are* bodies insofar as we *dwell* in them; and we *have* bodies insofar as we *focus* on them. We are embodied.

This structure of indwelling and reflection exists not only between the self and the body, but also within the self. We dwell in the unity of the whole self when we are functioning well and (pre)occupied with extrapsychic events. But at times we also turn our attention to ourselves (not just our bodies), and focus on the self-as-object. This reflexive analysis "breaks up" the self's unity, and we experience complexity and division within the self, sometimes very painfully.

The really difficult question is how far the process of stripping the self can go before the self is lost. Memory, a central theme in Augustine's *Confessions*, certainly plays a key role here. I may stop playing tennis, and become a former player, but if I should then forget that I had ever played, I would lose a part of my past, a part of myself. This is a negative way of making the positive point that memory is essential to our sense of self. Beyond everything else we have considered, it must be recognized that this sense of self is rooted, held, maintained in memory. As the wildly frequent cases of amnesia in soap opera plots amusingly remind us, without memory there would be no concrete, historical self, no cohesive unity-identity-whole that we experience; there would be no stream, only unconnected flickers of consciousness. Only through memory expressed in some kind of narrative (rarely a formal autobiography) does the ongoing, historical process of self-creation cohere in a sense of self.[35]

We have traced the self from Freud through several transitional figures to contemporary object-relations theorists and self psychologists. The historical pattern is definitely one of increasing prominence of the self—from implicit to explicit, from taken for granted to taken as central. The further we pursued the trail the closer we came to a psychoanalytic conception of the self that is clearly compatible with my theory of the dynamic, embodied, dipolar self ("I" and "me") fundamentally desiring *to be a self* and *to move beyond the self* in relationship. In these psychoanalytic conceptions we discovered valuable models for understanding the various ways (both healthy and distorted) in which the developing self-as-object takes shape—optimally in the real or true self grounded in supportive object-relationships. I conclude by noting the dialectical circularity in self-object relationships: the true self both emerges from supportive object-relationships and also gives rise to ever more expansive relationships.

Chapter 5

Self-Transcendence, the True Self, and Self-Love

DESIRE FOR SELF-TRANSCENDENCE

My basic understanding of the self is rooted in the premise that every person has a radical desire to reach out, to move beyond, to transcend the self. This drive is so basic and all-encompassing that it includes in some way all the specific drives and more: Freud's pleasure drive, Adler's power drive, and especially Frankl's drive for meaning. This radical desire for self-transcendence is at the source of everything that is specifically human, and is realized in every genuine instance of creative understanding, critical judging, responsible deciding, and generous loving. Authentic human realization is a self-transcending realization achieved through these specifically human activities. From a theological perspective, the drive for self-transcendence is the divine life within the human person, and its realization culminates in a personal relationship with God who is Truth and Goodness and Love. Henri Nouwen expresses the various dimensions of self-transcendence through the image of "reaching out." For him, the Christian spiritual life consists of three constant movements of reaching out: to ourselves (from loneliness to solitude), to others (from hostility to hospitality), and to God (from illusion to prayer).[1]

As we noted in Chapter 2, self-transcendence as a criterion of personal authenticity stands in complete opposition to both self-sacrifice and self-fulfillment, as these are commonly understood.

Self-transcendence stands over against self-sacrifice understood as a denial, renunciation, abnegation, or any other negation of the true self. Without a powerful, authentic self, there is little self-transcendence. At the same time, self-transcendence stands in firm opposition to any meaning of self-fulfillment which focuses on the self as a collection of wishes to be fulfilled. In contrast, the experience of self-transcendence supports the gospel's paradoxical view that authentic self-realization results not from a self-centered effort to fulfill one's every wish, but from a movement beyond oneself in an attempt to realize the good of others. Victor Frankl makes this point clearly in *Man's Search for Meaning*: "Human existence is essentially self-transcendence rather than self-actualization. Self-actualization is not a possible aim at all, for the simple reason that the more a man would strive for it, the more he would miss it." One is actualized or fulfilled, he says, only to the extent that one is committed to life's meaning: "Self-actualization cannot be attained if it is made an end in itself, but only as a side effect of self-transcendence."[2]

Indeed, such realization of the self through transcendence is actually a form of self-fulfillment. However, it is a fulfillment of the fundamental desire for meaning, truth, value, and love characteristic of personal beings. While its fulfillment in self-transcendence brings a sense of peaceful happiness, the very nature of this basic human desire defies any self-centered striving for happiness through fulfillment. In fact, the fulfillment proper to the radical personal desire for self-transcendence can require that one "empty" oneself in the sense of sacrificing not the self, but the fulfillment of otherwise legitimate interests of the self.[3]

Self-transcendence occurs, as I suggested in Chapter 2, in our effective response to the radical desire of the human spirit for meaning, truth, value, and love—a radical desire that is, at bottom, always a desire for God. The desire for understanding seeks meaning in our experience through questions for intelligence. These can be the practical questions of the home or office, the theoretical questions of the study or laboratory, the artistic questions of the stage or studio, or the philosophical-religious questions of the classroom or chapel. We seek meaning, but not just any meaning. For, once attained, meaning is critically scrutinized by the desire for truth. We seek evidence to support the meaning. Is it really so? This demand for verification is driven by questions for reflection heading toward realistic judgment. When we affirm meaning as true, with varying degrees of probability, we claim to be moving from thinking about the world to actually knowing it. Realistic judging, of course, is neither rash nor obsessed with certitude.

When experiencing, understanding, and judging occur within a practical pattern of value oriented toward action, there follows the further moral question for deliberation: given my judgment of the situation and required action, what am I going to do about it? Will I meet the demand of conscience by deciding to act in accord with my best judgment? Following Freud, many authors contrast conscience and desire. For example, Robert Kegan speaks of "Freud's hapless infantile ego, appearing to be a player in personality but in reality swamped by the contending forces of conscience and desire."[4] My interpretation, by focusing on radical desire and mature conscience, identifies desire and conscience: conscience *is* the radical desire for self-transcendence. In other words, conscience, as I have argued elsewhere, is nothing other than the self-as-subject striving for value.[5]

Finally, this practical questioning is permeated by a matrix of affectivity which must be strong enough to support the required action against the forces of conflicting interests. What, in the last analysis, am I going to commit myself to in love? Thus, every achievement of creative understanding, realistic judgment, responsible choice, and generous love is an instance of self-transcendence. Among all the possible realizations of human potential, such cognitive, moral, affective, and religious self-transcendence is *the* criterion of authentic self-realization, of the true self.

This then, is the structure of the desire for self-transcendence: questions for intelligence, reflection, and deliberation embodying the desire, and their responding operations of understanding, judging, and deciding which realize it. Because it is conscious, it also delineates the self by specifying distinct levels of consciousness: empirical, intelligent, rational, and responsible or existential—all interrelated as successive phases in the unfolding of the single desire of the human spirit for self-transcendence. From bodily nerves and psychic images, through sensitivity and intelligence, to free choice and love, the radical desire for self-transcendence unifies the self in its heuristic dynamism and integrates it in its realization.

In addition to cognitive self-transcendence, then, there is also affective self-transcendence. According to Lonergan's view, one is affectively self-transcendent when the isolation of the individual is broken and one spontaneously acts not just for self but also for the good of others. Affective self-transcendence thus grounds the real possibility of achieving moral self-transcendence in decisions to act for value. And, finally, beyond cognitive, affective, and moral self-transcendence, there is the possibility of religious self-transcendence. Lonergan says that a person's capacity and desire for self-transcendence meets joyful fulfillment when "religious conversion transforms the existential subject into a subject in love, a subject held, grasped, possessed, owned through a total and so an other-worldly love."[6] We will see more on this in our later discussion of conversion in Chapter 7.

So radical and thoroughgoing, indeed, is the desire for self-transcendence that we can complement the earlier affirmation that this desire is God within us by also identifying the radical desire with the self-as-subject. However, because the self-as-subject is never separate from the self-as-object, and because God is transcendent as well as immanent, this threefold identification of the radical desire for self-transcendence, God within us, and the self-as-subject is not pure and simple but ambiguous and complex. We shall return to this point in our consideration of Merton's true self.

This analysis of the desire for self-transcendence constitutes my fundamental understanding of the dynamic human person. It is important to note that this single concept of self-transcendence includes what psychologists as diverse as Freud and Piaget recognize as the two great yearnings of the human person: the desire for separation, differentiation, and autonomy on the one hand, and the desire for attachment, integration, and relationship on the other; that is, the desire *to be a self,* a center of strength, and the desire to reach beyond, *to transcend the self* in relationship. These two elements of the fundamental desire, the drive to be a self and the dynamism to transcend the self, are inextricably linked: separation *and* attachment, differentiation *and* integration, autonomy *and* relationship.

Self-transcendence, in short, is a radically interpersonal, relational reality. Outside of relationship there is no self. And this relational understanding of self-transcendence specifies the goal of pastoral counseling and spiritual direction: relational autonomy.

Pastoral counseling and spiritual direction are aimed at empowering persons to realize ever greater self-transcendence in their lives. To a great degree, this means helping people to liberate themselves from the countless defense mechanisms and other distortions of the personality that constitute a drag on the desire for self-transcendence. The concrete, historical person has a desire to transcend the self, but also has very real limitations. The task of pastoral counseling and spiritual direction is to deal with those limitations in order to increase the probability of self-transcendence in individual lives.

Having made reference to religious self-transcendence just a few paragraphs back, this is an appropriate point to complete our consideration of the self by examining Thomas Merton's notion of the true self of religious experience.

MERTON'S TRUE SELF

Thomas Merton (1915–1968)—Trappist monk, poet, and peace and justice advocate—placed the true self at the center of his teaching on the Christian life. We will consider key aspects of Merton's extraordinary life as illustrations in our chapter on conversion, but now we focus on his teaching in order to expand our interpretation of the self to the explicit dimension of Christian spirituality. In Chapter 4 we saw a psychological version of the true self in Guntrip's object-relations theory; here we will consider Merton's theological version, and then integrate it with Lonergan's self-as-subject within the framework of self-transcendence.

"For me," writes Merton in his 1949 *Seeds of Contemplation,* "to be a saint means to be myself." Sanctity consists of "finding out who I am and of discovering my true self." Unfortunately, "Every one of us is shadowed by an illusory person: a false self...who wants to exist outside the radius of God's will and God's love—outside of reality and outside of life." Though an illusion, the false self is, for most of us, *the* subjective reality. And this, for Merton, is the root sin, that the false self, "the self that exists only in my own egocentric desires, is the fundamental reality of life to which everything else in the universe is ordered." Thus the truth of life is paradoxical: "In order to become myself I must cease to be what I always thought I wanted to be, and in order to find myself I must go out of myself, and in order to live I must die." And the paradox of life is the paradox of love. Because God is love, a person "cannot enter into the deepest center of himself and thus pass through that center into God, unless he is able to pass entirely out of himself and empty himself to other people in the purity of a selfless love." For, as Merton writes, "love is my true identity. Selflessness is my true self. Love is my true character. Love is my name." For Merton, then, the spiritual "bottom line" is the true self: "If I find Him, I will find myself and if I find my true self I will find Him." But to reach the true self we must escape the prison of the false self.[7]

A dozen years later, in his 1961 *New Seeds of Contemplation*, Merton characterizes the false self as the superficial consciousness of the external self, irreducibly opposed to the "deep transcendent self that awakens only in contemplation." Merton also designates the superficial "I" of the external self as our empirical self, our individuality, our ego. He continues his explicitly theological interpretation by asserting that this external, empirical self is not "the hidden and mysterious person in whom we subsist before the eyes of God." In contemplation occurs "the awakening of the unknown 'I' that is beyond observation and reflection," and thus the discovery that the "I" of the external self is really "not I." Christian meanings of sin and grace are intrinsic to this interpretation. Because of the "fall," we are alienated from our inner self, the image of God in which we are created. To be "born in sin" means that we come into the world with a false self from which our true inner self must be saved by God's grace.[8]

Given this description of the true and false selves in terms of the spatial images of inner and outer, we still need a more precise explanation of their nature and relationship. Sometimes, for example, Merton speaks of the true self as existing, but hidden, in need of discovery. At other times he says we must, together with God, create our true self. Indeed, despite the clear theological thrust of his true self/false self distinction, Merton's other descriptive characterizations of the self, though related and similar, are not identical—for example, the empirical, external, alienated, illusory, narcissistic, and neurotic selves have somewhat different meanings from the false self—and should not necessarily be understood theologically.[9] An explanatory framework is needed to interpret the various sets of distinctions Merton draws within the self. An important clue to such an explanatory understanding is contained in Merton's 1959 study on contemplation, "The Inner Experience."

Merton highlights the wholeness of the inner self by affirming that it is "not a part of our being, like a motor in a car." It is, rather, "our entire substantial reality itself, on its highest and most personal and most existential level." The inner self, Merton explains, is "like life, and it is life: it is our spiritual life when it is most alive." Because it is a fundamental form of life, it "evades every concept that tries to seize hold of it with full possession," but "every deeply spiritual experience, whether religious or moral, or even artistic, tends to have in it something of the presence of the interior self." Indeed, the life of the inner self can communicate "a new life to the intelligence in which it lives, so that it becomes a living awareness of itself."[10]

This characterization of the inner, true self suggests a direct relationship to Lonergan's self-as-subject and radical desire for self-transcendence, and thus the possibility of an explanatory understanding of Merton's true self beyond descriptive spatial images. We can take the above points in reverse order. First, "a living awareness of itself" present in "every deeply spiritual experience" clearly points to the self-as-subject, the conscious, experienced presence of the self to itself which is "beyond observation and reflection," and "evades every concept that tries to seize hold of it." Second, "our spiritual life when it is most alive," our entire being "on its highest and most personal and most existential level" points directly to the self as structured by its radical desire for self-transcendence, unfolding on successive levels of consciousness, with the highest level of responsible or existential consciousness subsuming the empirical, intelligent, and rational levels.

This linking of the true self with both the desire for self-transcendence and the self-as-subject reflects our earlier identification of the radical desire for self-transcendence with the self-as-subject. Further, Merton's linking of the true self with the discovery of God reflects our earlier suggestion connecting the desire for self-transcendence with God's presence within us. Now, at the subject-pole, or, as Merton would say, the self's deepest center, we can integrate: the true self, the self-as-subject, the radical desire for self-transcendence, and God within us. This interior complex can be *experienced*, but only hinted at, never fully captured, in observation, conceptualization, or verbalization. At its best, traditional Christian language has used the words "spirit" and "soul" to refer to this dynamic interior complex. Of course, these words have also been degraded in various ways— dualism perhaps being the most frequent and pernicious.

Identification of the true self with the desire for self-transcendence allows us to understand how Merton can sometimes speak of the true self as existing, though hidden, and sometimes as needing to be created. We can affirm that the true self exists as the desire for self-transcendence, but is still to be fully created in the sense of an actually self-transcending person. In contrast, the false self is the person insofar as he or she is failing to respond to the self's most radical desire. In explanatory terms, then, Merton's true self as actualized is the self fully alive on the highest level of responsible, existential consciousness, reaching out beyond itself. Of course, self-transcendence in its fullest sense, and thus the true self in its fullest sense, is the result of conversion, in its cognitive, affective, moral, and religious dimensions, which we will consider in Chapter 7. There we will complete our reflection on Merton's true self by considering the transcendent self of religious conversion. At this point, however, we may note that the discovery of God in the true self is, as Anne Carr puts it, the "paradox of desire that ceases to be desire."[11]

We may conclude our present consideration of Merton's true self by referring back to this section's opening remarks about Guntrip, Merton, and Lonergan. It should be clear now that in contrast to the *structural* character of Guntrip's psychological understanding of the true self, Merton's theological version is heavily *moral-religious* in character. Lonergan's methodological interpretation of the self is *both structural and moral-religious,* and can thus integrate a psychological view like Guntrip's with a theological view like Merton's. This is precisely the orientation Charles Taylor advocates in his insistence on the necessity of connecting the self and the good.[12] Now that we have considered the desire for self-transcendence and the true self, we are in a position to examine the notoriously difficult issue of self-love.

SELF-LOVE

Few notions about the Christian life can contend with "self-love" for the designation of "most puzzling." We are told that we should love our neighbors as ourselves (Lk 10:27). Jesus also said that if we are to follow him, we must renounce ourselves (Mt 16:24). The point, surely, is not that we should renounce our neighbors, but what is it? How should we understand these lessons?[13] How can we both love and renounce ourselves? Most basically, what exactly does it mean to love oneself? Before attempting an answer to these puzzling questions, we should consult with another post-Freudian psychoanalytical theorist who has dealt with self-love explicitly, Erich Fromm.

Fromm starts with the fact that in much of Western thought—he refers to thinkers as different as Calvin and Freud—while it is considered virtuous to love others, it is sinful to love oneself. Love and self-love are seen as mutually exclusive; the more there is of one the less of the other. In this view self-love is the same as selfishness.[14]

In contrast, Fromm's approach is to make a radical distinction between self-love and selfishness, to regard them as opposites. Genuine love, says Fromm, "implies care, respect, responsibility, and knowledge." It is an "active striving for the growth and happiness of the loved person, rooted in one's capacity to love." Love of others and love of self go together. In Fromm's view, *the affirmation of one's own life, happiness, growth, freedom is rooted in one's capacity to love*, i.e., in care, respect, responsibility, and knowledge."[15]

This genuine self-love is exactly the opposite of selfishness. Interested only in themselves, selfish people see others and the world for what they can get out of them, want everything for themselves, and have no respect for the dignity of others or interest in their needs. Selfish people are basically unable to love anyone, including themselves. Though they appear to love themselves, says Fromm, they actually hate themselves. Again, though selfish people seem to care too much for themselves, in reality they are unsuccessfully attempting to compensate for failing to care for their *real* selves, as Fromm puts it.[16]

In sum, for Fromm, love is a basic affirmation of persons as incarnations of "essentially human qualities." Love of individual persons implies love of humanity, but only in and through individuals. Therefore, concludes Fromm, "my own self must be as much an object of my love as another person."[17]

We can take some clues from Fromm as we attempt to understand self-love in terms of self-transcendence. First, Fromm notes that selfish people fail to care for their *real* selves. This suggests that we should look to the self-as-subject in its dynamism for transcendence as a key to understanding self-love. At the same time, if the affirmation of one's own growth and happiness is rooted in one's capacity to love, to actively strive for the growth and happiness of others, it may be misleading to speak of one's self as an *object* of one's own love.

The distinction between healthy self-love and destructive selfishness lies precisely in self-transcendence, in the distinction between self-as-subject and self-as-object. We love ourselves in an authentic way by loving others. Loving others is loving ourselves because acting for the true good of others (their growth, happiness) is acting for our own true good (realization of our capacity for self-transcendence). This is loving ourselves-as-subjects in the act of loving others. To love ourselves as we love our neighbors is, as the gospel puts it, to love our neighbors as ourselves. In contrast, selfishness is the attempt to love ourselves-as-objects, to fulfill our every want and wish. The self the gospel calls us to renounce is the false self—the egocentric self-interests that obstruct the self-transcending love of others and ourselves that we are called to. We renounce the false self in order to love the true self-as-subject in and through its very reaching out to love others. Like consciousness, in which the self is known as subject in the same act that knows objects, authentic self-love is not a reflexive, second act of loving the self as object, but an interior dimension (subject) of the one act of loving an other (object). Attempting to love the self in any other way (as object) is certain to fail, is doomed to selfishness. Like happiness, self-love is elusive: the more we seek it, the more it escapes us. Both happiness and self-love are realized only in self-transcending love of others.

Chapter 6

The Developing Self: A Pastoral Counseling Guide

One of the most obvious and important facts about the desiring self is that it changes. Much of the self's change is what we call personal development. We watch babies become children, then adolescents, then young women and young men. We have experienced this process of development ourselves. We know that it involves much more than physical maturity, important as that is. Developmental psychologists have delineated patterns of this "more" in various basic dimensions: affective (Erik Erikson), cognitive (Jean Piaget), moral (Lawrence Kohlberg), faith (James Fowler), and even the "self" itself (Robert Kegan). In this chapter we will track and integrate the main lines of these developmental patterns in order to appreciate the reality of the desiring self as concretely as possible. As we do so, I will highlight how the very meaning of development in these patterns is self-transcendence. We shall see how each transition in the course of development is an instance of self-transcendence, a new self moving beyond the former self. We shall also see how the basic, overall process—indeed, the normative course—of development is a movement from radical egocentrism in infancy toward ever greater self-transcendence in adult life.

In order to be truly helpful to their clients, pastoral counselors and spiritual directors need to understand personal development so they can more accurately discern where their clients presently are in the course of life and also have a more critical and precise grasp—psychologically and theologically—of development's authentic direction and goal. Toward that end of identifying the desiring self's developmental possibilities, this chapter will present a general guide map, offering an overview of the territory and marking some of its notable features. We will begin with a detailed consideration of infancy, because it is there that the desire for self-transcendence that pastoral helpers want to promote in adults first emerges.

THE CHILD: TRUST—BREAKING THE BONDS OF EGOCENTRISM

From Egocentrism to Objectivity

Egocentrism is a philosophical concept that has been popularized in cognitive developmental psychology by Jean Piaget. Basically, of course, it means self-centeredness, just the opposite of self-transcendence. Applied to adults, the term "egocentric" is judgmentally negative. But applied to young children, it is descriptively neutral. We expect young children to be self-centered. That is just the way they are, in their thinking and thus in their behavior. They are incapable of anything else. The word becomes an expression of censure with adults because we expect more of adults. We expect more because we implicitly assume that "growing up" involves a movement away from egocentrism toward self-transcendence. This chapter will make that assumption explicit and bring it into critical understanding.

In Chapter 4 we noted in the context of object-relations theory and self psychology the thesis of self/object differentiation in the infant. Despite differences among developmentalists such as Margaret Mahler and Daniel Stern, the basic point shared by the various theorists is that this differentiation exists by the end of the infant's second year. Now we shall consider the major contribution of Swiss psychologist Jean Piaget to this important discussion.

Piaget has delineated a course of cognitive development beginning in infancy and moving through key stages of childhood and adolescence into adulthood. The four major stages are sensorimotor, preoperational, concrete operational, and formal operational. We will follow this course at appropriate points throughout this chapter. But the basic pattern of this developmental course is

PIAGET COGNITIVE	ERIKSON AFFECTIVE	KEGAN SELF	KOHLBERG MORAL	FOWLER FAITH	LONERGAN CONVERSIONS
	8) Integrity/Despair Widom		7) Religious	6) Universalizing	Religious
	7) Generativity/Stagnation Care		6) Universal Principles	5) Conjunctive	Critical Moral
Contextual-Dialectic	6) Intimacy/Isolation Love	5) Interindividual	5) Social Contract	4) Individuative-Reflective	Affective
			4¹/₂) Relativist		
Full Formal	5) Identity/Confusion Fidelity	4) Institutional	4) Authority-Social order		Moral
Early Formal		3) Interpersonal	3) Interpersonal Concordance	3) Synthetic-Conventional	
Concrete	4) Industry/Inferiority Competence	2) Imperial	2) Instrumental-Relativist	2) Mythic-Literal	
Preoperational	3) Initiative/Guilt Purpose	1) Impulsive	1) Punishment-Obedience	1) Intuitive-Projective	
	2) Autonomy/Shame, Doubt Will				
Sensorimotor	1) Trust/Mistrust Hope	0) Incorporative	0) Amoral	0) Undifferentiated	

FIGURE 1: Relationships Among Developmental Patterns and Conversions

established during infancy: from an initial undifferentiated egocentrism to a more and more differentiated objectivity.

The basic features of Piaget's biologically rooted theory of cognitive development are the interrelated dynamics of organization and adaptation. Organization is the invariant process of structuring intelligence into various forms as development goes forward. "Adaptation is an equilibrium between assimilation and accommodation."[1] It is an interplay, a *pas de deux*. As assimilation, intelligence incorporates the data of experience into its structures. But assimilation can never be pure because new data require intelligence to modify its structure in order to accommodate to the environment. Indeed, assimilation and accommodation go hand in hand in every adaptational act: every assimilation of an object to the structures of intelligence involves a simultaneous accommodation of the structures to the object. Thus, by moving dialectically toward an equilibrium, assimilating and accommodating activities constantly create and recreate the structures of intelligence, and, thereby, the shape of the subject's world.

At the beginning of the infant's sensorimotor stage, assimilation and accommodation are undifferentiated, and thus an object (for example, the mother's breast) and the activity to which the object is assimilated (such as sucking) form an indivisible experience. As a result, self and object are merged in every infantile action, and the distinction between assimilation and accommodation does not yet exist.[2] Piaget points out that to the extent that infantile "activity is undifferentiated from the things it constantly assimilates to itself it remains unaware of its own subjectivity; the external world therefore begins by being confused with the sensations of a self unaware of itself, before the two factors become detached from one another and are organized correlatively."[3] As John Flavell has expressed Piaget's perspective on the infant, "the egocentric subject is a kind of solipsist aware of neither self nor solipsism."[4] Through what Piaget calls an apparently paradoxical mechanism, "it is precisely when the subject is most self-centered that he knows himself the least, and it is to the extent that he discovers himself that he places himself in the universe and constructs it by virtue of that fact."[5] Thus, if egocentrism means the absence of self-perception and objectivity, cognitive acquisition of objects entails self-perception because, as we noted in Chapter 3, in contrast to consciousness, in self-perception the self is an object to itself. Pastoral counselors and spiritual directors know all too well, of course, that infants have no exclusive rights on self-centeredness as an obstacle to self-knowledge. Unhappily, the pattern repeats itself in various ways at all the stages of life. Our desire for self-transcendence may be radical, but our clinging to the center is stubbornly persistent.

Piaget has described the infant's two-year development out of profound egocentrism as a "miniature Copernican revolution." At the beginning the newborn grasps everything to its body, but at the end—as language and thought begin to appear—the young child has become one of the many entities in an external universe it has constructed. During this period of practical intelligence, development through several substages completely transforms the infant's initial position in relation to the external world. "The self is at the center of reality to begin with for the very reason that it is not aware of itself, while the external world will become objectified to the degree that the self builds itself as a function of subjective or internal activity."[6] Starting from egocentricity, consciousness develops through the construction of an objective universe to an internal life localized in the young child's body and contrasted to the external world. So, with simultaneous centrifugal and centripetal processes, there occurs a gradual objectification of external reality and a greater self-perception, with the self seen as an object among other objects.[7]

From the child's cognitive relationship with this new external world evolve the basic concepts of object, space, causality, and time. The most fundamental of these, presupposed by the others, is the object concept. During the infant's first year, "out of sight" is equivalent to "out of reality," but gradually the infant begins to grasp not just sensory pictures but permanent, substantive objects. Mommy continues to exist, even when she cannot be seen. This is the beginning of the shift from an egocentric chaos to a structured cosmos.[8] Many more significant cognitive advances will be made in the following years, which will relativize even the Copernican revolution of the sensorimotor period. But the importance of the gains made during the sensorimotor period—especially the permanent object—should not be minimized. Indeed, the appearance of the permanent object is intimately linked to the psychoanalytic "object choice." As Piaget explains it, "The affective 'object choice' which psychoanalysis contrasts with narcissism is...correlated with the

intellectual construction of the object, just as narcissism is correlated with lack of differentiation between the external world and
the self." Of course the construction of the object is only half of the
story: the perception of the self is its necessary subjective correlative. Piaget reminds us that the "narcissism" of psychoanalysis is a
"narcissism without Narcissus, that is, without any sense of personal awareness as such."[9] We should be clear that this newly perceived "self" is the self-as-object. The conscious self-as-subject is
present from the beginning, but without any reflective awareness of
itself. The emergence of reflective awareness introduces the issues
connected with what Erik Erikson terms "autonomy." We will consider this shortly, but first we turn to the initial crisis in the Eriksonian life cycle, trust. Before leaving Piaget, however, I should
emphasize that we lingered on him in this section because the basic
thrust (if not all the details) of his thesis on egocentrism and objectivity is at the heart of this book's premise: the person's radical
desire for self-transcendence. In infancy we see the radical nature
of this desire in a strikingly clear way. In later years our response to
this desire makes us the kind of concrete, historical selves we gradually become, but in infancy this radical desire creates the very
dipolar, reflective self ("I" and "me") that each of us is.

Trust and Hope

While cognitive self/object differentiation is occurring, the
infant is also experiencing the first affective crisis Erikson specifies
in the psychosocial life cycle—the struggle to work out a balance
favoring basic trust over against mistrust. By "trust" Erikson means
a "pervasive attitude toward oneself and the world derived from the
experiences of the first year of life,...an essential trustfulness of others as well as a fundamental sense of one's own trustworthiness."[10]
For Erikson, achievement of this trust is primarily a function of the
quality of maternal care, the same point we saw emphasized by
object-relations theorists. Mothers, he says, "create a sense of trust
in their children by that kind of administration which in its quality
combines sensitive care of the baby's individual needs and a firm
sense of personal trustworthiness within the trusted framework of
their culture's life style."[11]

The successful resolution of this crisis, like all those to follow, is never a case of all or nothing, but a favorable balance of trust. Total victory over mistrust would result in an inappropriately pure, and therefore naive, trust. Even in the best circumstances, the infant experiences a sense of inner division, deprivation, and abandonment that basic trust must overcome throughout life. Indeed, the particular strength or virtue proper to infancy is hope, "the enduring belief in the attainability of fervent wishes, in spite of the dark urges and rages which mark the beginning of existence." If life is to be sustained, says Erikson, "hope must remain, even where confidence is wounded, trust impaired."[12] For the adult, serious loss of hope means regression into a state of virtual lifelessness. Pastoral counselors know that religious affiliation is no sure protection against such loss.

In the larger picture of the life cycle trust "forms the basis in the child for a sense of identity which will later combine a sense of being 'all right,' of being oneself, and of becoming what other people trust one will become."[13] And by receiving from its mother, Erikson says, the infant "also develops the necessary groundwork 'to get to be' the giver—that is, to identify with [its mother] and eventually to become a giving person,"[14] to become, in the language of our thesis, a self-transcending person. Thus it is in infancy that trust and hope effectively break the bonds of affective egocentrism. As in Mary's case, however, trust is not always sufficiently established. Mary is painfully aware of the inadequacies in her relationship with her mother, inadequacies that extend back as far as Mary can remember.

Self: Differentiation and Integration

Whereas Piaget and Erikson focus respectively on the specific cognitive and affective dimensions of personal development, Robert Kegan concentrates on delineating the fundamental unity of the developing self that lies beneath and integrates cognition and affectivity as well as subject and object. Kegan discovers this fundamental unity in the meaning-making activity that constitutes the very motion of the self's development.

Kegan works from a neo-Piagetian constructive-developmental perspective, but shifts the focus of differentiation and integration from cognition to the prior reality of the self. From this perspective,

Kegan views the self's radical developmental activity as both the creation of the object (differentiation) and the subject's relating to it (integration). Thus from a lifelong process of development emerges a series of ever more complex differentiations of self from the world, what Kegan calls "successive triumphs of 'relationship to' rather than 'embeddedness in'."[15]

While Piaget and Erikson are concerned with the gradual development of cognitive and affective object relations in the infant, Kegan reaches for the "more basic phenomenon [underlying cognition and affectivity], the evolutionary transition from an undifferentiated state to the first equilibrium" between self and other or between subject and object. With an object-relation balance established by eighteen months, a pattern of development is set as "an activity of equilibration, of preserving or renegotiating the balance between what is taken as subject or self and what is taken as object or other." The developmental process is a continual differentiation from the subject-pole, transference to the object-pole, and integration of subject and object poles. This developmental activity is clearly cognitive (for example, the infant's ability to relate to absent objects), but it is also intrinsically affective, the felt experience of motion (for example, the infant's protest at separation from its mother). By locating the fundamental ground of self in decentration, Kegan specifies the source of emotion as the "phenomenological experience of evolving—of defending, surrendering, and reconstructing a center."[16] Since decentration from embeddedness to greater relatedness is always experienced as a loss of self (center), it is accompanied by anxiety and depression. As the balance shifts to the new self, there is anger and repudiation of the former self, now at the object-pole. Only when the new balance is fully established can the old self be positively reappropriated. Guidance through the adult negotiation of this process is a central task of counselors and directors.

As a result of the decentering development during infancy, the self emerges from embeddedness in its reflexes. At the beginning the infant does not have but *is* its reflexes. But in a radical transformation of its deep structure, the self disembeds itself from its reflexes, which now become the object of a new organizing self. Thus by the end of infancy the self no longer is its reflexes, but *has* them at its object-pole, and therefore is not subject to them. This escape from the primordial incorporative stage of infancy does constitute a radical transformation of the self, but it is only the beginning of a multistage development. We will trace the continuing differentiation and integration of subject and object throughout the lifespan with Kegan in later sections.

I have emphasized the years of infancy because this is the period in which the pattern of development from egocentrism to self-transcendence is established. As we have seen, this pattern occurs during infancy: 1) in the cognitive dimension with the self/object distinction and relation as assimilation and accommodation are differentiated and integrated; 2) in the affective dimension with the emergence of a favorable ratio of trust over mistrust; and 3) in the deep self structure with the liberation of the self from embeddedness in its reflexes.

The Impulsive Self: Autonomy, Initiative, and Industry

If the first psychosocial crisis of trust vs. mistrust highlights the "transcendence" side of the self-transcendence equation in the issue of relationship, the succeeding crises of childhood identified by Erikson tend to emphasize the "self" side of self-transcendence in the continuing construction of an independent individual that gradually becomes more and more capable of moving beyond itself. These three crises of childhood, which correspond to Freud's anal, phallic, and latent stages respectively, are *autonomy* vs. shame and doubt, *initiative vs.* guilt, and *industry vs.* inferiority. From their successful resolutions the self is strengthened in will, purpose, and competence.

Every parent who has experienced the defying "No" of the "terrible twos" knows what Erikson means by the willful "autonomy" of the self-asserting toddler. I like to refer to this strength as "independence" rather than "autonomy" because, although a necessary virtue, it should not be confused with the autonomy of the mature adult. The strength specific to the toddler is unbalanced, as it only can be at this stage. As difficult as this defiant independence is for parents, it is recognized as age appropriate, and as a promise of future character. The adolescent version of independence—as challenging as that can be for parents—is also recognized as developmentally necessary, but when we see stubborn counterdependent willfulness in an adult we recognize not maturity but inappropriate exaggeration or perhaps even mildly pathological aberration: childish "independence" that has never struck the mature balance of *mutual* autonomy. Mary, for example, asserts an independent, even stubborn, willfulness, but her lack of truly adult autonomy is revealed in her need to both rebel against authority and fuse with partners.

Paired against autonomy in Erikson's schema is shame, which Fowler has recently highlighted, in relation to the self, as "painful self-consciousness, alienation, and inner self-division." Unlike guilt, which is about something we do, shame is directly about the self: "the awareness of the self as disclosed to others, or to the self, as being defective, lacking, or inadequate...and, at worst, contemptible." Shame can be brutally destructive (splitting the self, as we have seen in object-relations theory), but in its healthy forms it also plays an essentially positive role "in the forming and maintenance of a sense of balance and worthiness in the emerging self," the beginnings of conscience.[17]

While autonomy is asserting itself in Erikson's schema, the young child who has emerged from the infantile embeddedness of the self in its reflexes is entering into Kegan's Impulsive stage, when it no longer *is* its reflexes but *has* them at the object-pole. But while freed from subjection to its reflexes, the new Impulsive self is embedded in and thus subject to its impulses and perceptions. Now the self *has* its reflexes but *is* its impulses and perceptions. The pre-schooler thus has no control of its perceptions and impulses, which, with no center to hold them together, are unorganized, always changing. The young child's lightning-fast shift from joyful delight to tantrum is probably the most powerful expression of this lack of control. The impulsive self cannot handle ambivalence.

Two or three years later the split within consciousness takes a decisive turn with the Eriksonian crisis of initiative vs. guilt. Here emerges the Freudian superego, what Erikson calls "the great governor of initiative." A radical division and estrangement is created within the self, and consciousness is never again the same. Parental rules are internalized, and now the child not only worries that parents will discover transgressions, but fears the guilt produced by "the 'inner voice' of self-observation, self-guidance, and self-punishment."[18] Later development notwithstanding, the superego remains a permanent aspect of the moral life, always to be dealt with. But if a balance favoring initiative ensues from this crisis, a foundation is laid for the development of an adult conscience. In such cases the positive values of a self-transcending conscience, not the negative prohibitions of a moralistic superego, come to dominate the moral life. That development is never easy, but its pain is the price of authentic adulthood. In the meantime, the internalized constraints of the superego rule the morality of childhood.

If play is the activity featured in the period of initiative, work—or at least preparation for work—moves to the center during the school period of industry. In all cultures at this stage, "children receive systematic instruction of some kind and learn eagerly from older children."[19] They also learn to win recognition by producing things.[20] The wisdom of life's ground plan, as Erikson puts it, arranges the coincidence of this psychosocial crisis of industry vs. inferiority with the Freudian psychosexual period of latency and the Piagetian cognitive stage of concrete operations. For while latency allows concentration on the issues of industry, the emergence and logical grouping of concrete operations constitutes the radical cognitive breakthrough that grounds the development of the period's proper strength, industrious competence: "the free exercise of dexterity and intelligence in the completion of tasks, unimpaired by infantile inferiority."[21]

During the periods of autonomy and initiative affective development is accompanied and supported by the development of what Piaget calls preoperational intellectual activity. Cognitively, this is essentially a period of transition and preparation. The key transition is from the external actions of sensorimotor practical intelligence to the internalized actions of genuine *thought*. This prepares the cognitive ground for the later breakthrough of organized internal actions that Piaget calls "operations." The major factors contributing to the transformation of this period are language and socialization. As both these elements slowly increase, the young child's thought is exposed to criticism from other perspectives. This critical discussion is gradually internalized, leading the child to look for evidence to support statements that were earlier merely asserted. Thus thought moves from intuition to a rudimentary kind of reflection. Despite Mary's affective difficulties during childhood, her strong interest in reading and music indicate healthy intellectual development in the early stages.

The Imperial Self and Concrete Thinking

At about this time begins the emergence of concrete operational thought, which marks a major point in the cognitive shift from egocentrism to a decentered objectivity. What were earlier merely isolated individual intuitions are now logical operations, organized and interrelated systematically in groupings. The essential characteristic of logical operations is reversibility; in arithmetic, for example, adding and then subtracting the same number, or multiplying and then dividing by the same number, takes us back to where we started. These powerful logical operations place the knowing self in a wholly new cognitive world of objective relations. By the time a youngster is ten or eleven, this transformation is complete, allowing the self to move beyond its own viewpoint and appreciate those of others. Even greater cognitive development is to come, but operational thought has effected a deep revolution in the preadolescent self, moving it into a world totally beyond the horizon of the preoperational child.

As the physical world is being conserved with the emergence of concrete operations, so too is conservation transforming internal experience and thereby creating an interior world unknown to the younger preoperational child. As a result, the school-age child can objectify its impulses as well as its perceptions, thus eliminating its earlier instability and establishing a more enduring self. As Kegan explains it, this transformation means that the self no longer *is* its impulses and perceptions but now *has* them at the object-pole. Now the disposition of the more stable self dominates the subject-pole, and the self is embedded in its needs, interests, and wishes. At this Imperial stage the child projects its embeddedness in its needs, interests, and wishes onto the other, making the other the means of fulfilling them. This manipulation occurs because while the child understands that others have their own needs, interests, and wishes, it does not yet have the ability to integrate them with its own or to share the other's feelings. That kind of empathic mutuality only comes with later development in perspective-taking.

On a more positive note, now that the Imperial self can control its impulses, it enjoys a significantly greater sense of agency and responsibility, all part of a dawning sense of one's own authority. With the greater power, freedom, and independence of agency, the child now appreciates that things do not just happen ("the glass broke"), but that he or she has something to do with what happens, and thus some responsibility for it. All of this development in the self's structure has direct impact on the child's moral life, to which we now turn.

Early Moral and Faith Development

Our chief guide as we examine development in the moral sphere will be Lawrence Kohlberg, who delineates six stages of moral reasoning, paired off on three levels: preconventional, conventional, and postconventional. By "conventional" Kohlberg means "conforming to and upholding the rules and expectations and conventions of society or authority just because they are society's rules, expectations, or conventions."[22] The key to moral reasoning development, then, is the self's socialization.

At the preconventional level, the child, with a concrete individual social perspective, does not really understand society's rules and expectations, which are therefore external. At Stage 1 the child with emerging concrete operations understands "good" and "bad" in terms of avoiding punishment, obeying for the sake of obeying, and not causing physical damage. Still egocentric in social perspective, the interests of others mean nothing to the young child at this stage. But as concrete operations develop, the older child's social perspective becomes capable of recognizing that others, too, have interests, and that interests often conflict. Doing the right thing at the second stage of Instrumental Relativism becomes a matter of acting in one's own interest, allowing others to act in theirs, and sometimes making deals of fair exchange. In Mary's case, of course, having a father who is emotionally distant and a mother who is a sparring partner is not especially conducive to this kind of development.

So, even from early to later childhood, we see in Kohlberg's analysis of moral development some real movement from an egocentrism focused on punishment and obedience to the self-transcendence of reflective perspective-taking and fair exchange. This development involves a move away from a preoccupation with physical consequences, black and white views of right and wrong, and punishment, toward greater awareness of the agent's intentions, relativism and diversity, and harm done to others or violations of rules. The development in this trend is real, but limited. Just as the period's radical breakthrough of operational thought is real cognitive development, but is limited by the intrinsic concreteness of the operations, so too is the period's development in moral reasoning limited by an excessive focus on the concrete interests of the self. The greater development we will see in adolescence is required to break the empirical chains of concrete reality. Before moving on to adolescence, though, we will complete our consideration of childhood with a look at faith development in this period.

As Kohlberg is our guide for moral development, James Fowler, whose analysis was inspired by the Piagetian-Kohlberg cognitive-structural approach, is our guide for development in the dimension of faith, or, as he sometimes calls it to stress its active character, "faithing." In Fowler's approach, faith is an interpreting of experience in terms of the ultimate conditions of existence, of one's relatedness to those "sources of power and values which impinge on life in a manner not subject to personal control."[23] Despite his cognitive-structural approach, Fowler affirms the whole self's involvement in "faithing"—the affective and evaluative as well as the cognitive dimensions. Because he focuses on the structural core of "faithing" (knowing and valuing) rather than the content of faith (knowledge and values), Fowler understands faith ("faithing") as a universal human reality that may, but need not, be religious in any explicit, conventional sense. As we proceed in the following sections, we will consider the six stages of faith Fowler has specified: (1) Intuitive-Projective, (2) Mythic-Literal, (3) Synthetic-Conventional, (4) Individuative-Reflective, (5) Conjunctive (Paradoxical-Consolidative), and (6) Universalizing. At this point we will consider only the first two stages, those characteristic of childhood.

During infancy Primal faith is undifferentiated from the trusting hope that Erikson designates as normative for this preconceptual and prelinguistic period. But as the symbolic function emerges during the preoperational stage, the young child begins to manifest the fantasy-filled, imitative characteristics of Intuitive-Projective faith. Because the child is so totally dependent on parents for love, security, and nurturance, they play a key role as authorities in the child's attempt to construct a meaningful world. Though still egocentric, the child's power of imagination (painfully terrifying as well as delightfully exciting) is essential to faith at this stage.

Through imagination, stories can now shape the child's efforts to grasp life's ultimate conditions. Deprived of a rich intimacy with her parents as a young girl, Mary found some comfort in her room with her books and music.

As the purposeful initiative of the play age gives way to the industrious competence of the school age, the new power of concrete operational thinking grounds the emergence of Mythic-Literal faith. Now the child is not simply influenced by stories, but has the ability to create its own stories, to narratize its experience. The same cognitive operations make it possible for the school-age child to appropriate the stories, beliefs, attitudes, and moral rules of the community, but the limitations of concrete operations also mean that this appropriation will be uncritical and literal. So, for example, while the ability to take the perspective of others results in a more personalized image of God than the young child has, that image bears the heavy anthropomorphism of the concrete imagination. Still, as limited as it is, this "faithing" is yet another evidence of the preadolescent's attempt to reach beyond itself, trying to interpret experience in terms of its limits. With Ana-Maria Rizzuto, Fowler emphasizes the importance of parental images in the child's construction of its God representation. It is not difficult for us to imagine the effect that Mary's strained parental relationships had on her image of God.[24]

THE ADOLESCENT:
SEARCHING FOR INDEPENDENT MEANING,
VALUES AND FAITH

Identity and Formal Thinking

Identity is the focus of Erikson's consideration of the entire lifespan, but it reaches its point of crisis in adolescence. As we saw in Chapter 3, Erikson's understanding of identity is "at once subjective and objective, individual and social." While it includes a subjective sense of sameness and continuity as an active, alive individual, it also has a social side in the expectations and traditional values of the community in which the young person seeks role integration. In adolescence everything from the young person's past seems to come together with the anticipated demands of the future to produce crisis: infantile and childhood identifications, new self-definitions, and irreversible role choices.[25] Now all the "samenesses and continuities relied on earlier are more or less questioned again, because of a rapidity of body growth which equals that of early childhood and because of the new addition of genital maturity." Adolescents, "faced with this physiological revolution within them and with tangible adult tasks ahead of them, are now primarily concerned with what they appear to be in the eyes of others as compared with what they feel they are, and with the question of how to connect the roles and skills cultivated earlier with the occupational prototypes of the day."[26]

Above all, adolescence is a "moratorium for the integration of the identity elements" specific to the earlier stages, an integration which must be realized in the new, larger, and more demanding context of society. As the infant needed to establish trust in itself and others, the adolescent needs to find people and ideas to have faith in, to be dedicated to. As the toddler knew itself as what it could freely will, the adolescent now must freely decide on an avenue of duty and service. As the young child flourished in imaginative play, the adolescent seeks "peers and leading, or misleading, elders who will give imaginative, if not illusory, scope to his aspirations...." As the school-age child desired to make something work well, the adolescent finds that the "choice of an occupation assumes a significance beyond the question of remuneration and status." Though always difficult, this period of identity integration will be less stormy for those adolescents whose gifts and training allow them easy access to the economic and technological world. Others less fortunate may become more explicitly ideological in their search for inspiration. And failure to find genuine social response to this search can result, says Erikson, in resistance "with the wild strength encountered in animals who are suddenly forced to defend their lives. For, indeed, in the social jungle of human existence, there is no feeling of being alive without a sense of identity."[27] Mary, unfortunately, knows this all too well.

Linked to this ideological seeking for an inner coherence and durable values is the specific strength that emerges from a successful resolution of the identity crisis: fidelity, "the ability to sustain loyalties freely pledged in spite of the inevitable contradictions of value systems." Erikson sees fidelity as the "opportunity to fulfill personal potentialities (including erotic vitality or its sublimation) in a context which permits the young person to be true to himself and true to significant others." The truth of fidelity verifies itself in many ways, according to Erikson: "A high sense of duty, accuracy, and veracity in the rendering of reality; the sentiment of truthfulness, as in sincerity and conviction; the quality of genuineness, as in authenticity; the trait of loyalty, of 'being true'; fairness to the rules of the game; and finally all that is implied in devotion—a freely given but binding vow, with the fateful implication of a curse befalling traitors." To stress how the fidelity of identity constitutes the very meaning of youthful life, Erikson cites the example of Hamlet. "When Hamlet, the emotional victim of his royal parents' faithlessness, poses the question, 'To be or not to be,' he demonstrates in word and deed that to him 'to be' is contingent on being loyal (to the self, to love, to the crown) and that the rest is death."[28]

The mutuality characteristic of adolescence is highlighted in the experience of "falling in love," which, according to Erikson, often involves "an attempt to arrive at a self-definition by seeing oneself reflected anew in an idealized as well as eroticized other."[29] We could ask for no better example of this than Mary's desperate longing for a husband. In this adolescent experience of "falling in love" we see a developing realization of self and its capacity for further self-transcendence in the very process of reaching out to another in mutuality.

In sum, the integration of an identity is a creative act of self-understanding that goes beyond everything one has been before.[30] In a very real sense, then, successful resolution of the identity crisis is the very essence of self-transcendence. We turn now, therefore, to the adolescent's expanding cognitive power for self-transcendence in formal operational thought.

The crisis of identity experienced in adolescence and the consolidation of identity achieved in later youth are rendered possible by the cognitive transformation that begins early in adolescence. Erikson points out that "the adolescent learns to grasp the flux of time, to anticipate the future in a coherent way, to perceive ideas and to assent to ideals, to take—in short—an *ideological* position for which the younger child is cognitively not prepared." We shall follow Piaget now, therefore, in tracking the integrated cognitive dimension of personal development that complements the affective dimension of identity, and grounds what Erikson calls a "*historical* perspective, which makes room not only for imaginative speculation about all that could have happened in the past," but also "a sense of the irreversibility of significant events" and a "deepening concern with the narrowing down of vast possibilities to a few alternatives...."[31] This historical perspective is what gives the self its concrete, narrative quality, what grounds *character.*

The adolescent, in Piaget's view, is a builder of systems and theories. Although the concrete operations of the child are systematic, they are focused on isolated problems. The child does not integrate solutions into general theories, nor does the child abstract common principles. In contrast, the adolescent, freed from the here and now limitations of the concrete, exploits the systematic qualities of operational thinking. As formal operations emerge, the adolescent begins to locate the real within the possible, not merely in the empirical. The adolescent's formal operational thinking is abstract: hypothetical-deductive, propositional, and combinatorial. Its operations are second degree operations; like algebra in contrast to arithmetic, it operates on the results of operations. It forms abstract propositions from the results of concrete operations, systematically combines all the possible variables, and works toward the logical justification of hypotheses. Piaget argues that its implicit structure is reflected explicitly in the integrated lattice-groups of mathematical logic. The new power of formal thinking brings together and transforms earlier strengths; it embodies the young child's fundamental wonder in a controlled manner, and continues the older child's concern for order, but opens it up to the hypothetical world of possibility.

This new cognitive power allows the adolescent to live not only in the present (to which the child is mostly bound), but also in a nonpresent, hypothetical world full of plans for the future, social as well as individual, just when the identity crisis is forcing the adolescent to look toward the possibilities of the adult world. But until formal thought actually meets the reality demands of the adult world, it retains its peculiar form of egocentrism, an egocentrism "manifested by belief in the omnipotence of reflection, as though the world should submit itself to idealistic schemes rather than to systems of reality."[32] We noted in Chapter 1 and will attend again in

Chapter 8 to Mary's strengths as well as her limitations in formal operational thinking.

The Interpersonal Self: Adolescent Moral and Faith Development

The cognitive transformation of adolescence makes possible a totally new dimension of interpersonal relations and, as a result, a new self. Whereas the child's Imperial self *was* its needs, the adolescent is able to transfer these needs to the object-pole, where it *has* them and is no longer subject to them. This new control of its needs allows the adolescent self to coordinate them with the needs of others, becoming mutual and empathic.[33] Shared feelings are the strength of the new Interpersonal self, but also its limitation, insofar as the self cannot reflect on this shared reality because it *is* this shared reality. Subject to its interpersonal matrix, the adolescent self experiences conflict as it is torn between different shared realities. The Interpersonal self is thus without the self-coherence essential to identity. Indeed, just as the Stage 2 self imperialized others for its own need-satisfaction, the Stage 3 Interpersonal self needs others to be a self. For the Interpersonal self, to lose a significant other is to lose its own self, to experience nothingness. It is not difficult to see Mary's intensely painful experiences as part of this deadly dynamic.

The adolescent self at the Interpersonal stage is the self that is moving into Kohlberg's conventional moral orientation. This is the developmental point when maintaining the expectations and rules of family, group, and nation is seen as good in itself. At the early adolescent's moral Stage 3, right behavior means pleasing or helping others—seeking their approval by being a "nice" girl or a "good" boy. Good intentions and conformity to social stereotypes of the good person become important. Preoccupation with one's own interests gives way to shared feelings, expectations, and agreements. We noted that Fowler sees Mary at this point of moral development, but it is a Stage 3 seriously complicated by counterdependent relationships. The older, Stage 4, adolescent assumes the social perspective of the system that defines roles and rules, viewing interpersonal relations in terms of their place in the social system. In this perspective, good behavior means not only doing one's duty and respecting authority, but also working to maintain the social order for its own sake.

The importance we have seen Erikson give to fidelity is reflected in Fowler's understanding of faith as the self moves into adolescence. Faith "must help provide a coherent and meaningful synthesis" of the complex and diverse involvements the self experiences as it moves beyond the family into a much larger world during adolescence. Faith's meaning is now certified by the authority of key persons, those who "count" in the self's eyes. This faithed meaning must ground not only one's identity but also one's ideological orientation and commitment. Despite the cognitive transformation that has already begun, the adolescent's thinking is not yet critical, so faith at this stage is mediated by symbols that are "dwelt in," as Polanyi would say, in a precritical or naive fashion. The interpersonal quality of Stage 3's Synthetic-Conventional faith is manifested in typical images of God, whose anthropomorphism has taken a personal rather than physical character—God is friend, companion, comforter, guide. Though Stage 3 faith makes its first appearance in and is characteristic of adolescence, Mary is an example of the many young and older adults who find a more or less comfortable home in Synthetic-Conventional faith. As we saw in Chapter 1, Mary constantly turns to God for guidance, but never blames God when things go wrong.

The Institutional Self and Moral Relativism

In later adolescence, when the crisis of identity may be reaching a resolution, there is the related possibility of a further transformation of self. As we have just seen with Kegan, the early adolescent Interpersonal self at Stage 3 *is* its relationships. With the creation of a coherent identity spanning all its relationships, however, the self is able to separate from its relationships. No longer divided among its relationships, the self has a sense of self-ownership. Because the self no longer *is* its relationships, but rather *has* them, the self is now, at the subject-pole, what Kegan calls a psychic institution. This Stage 4 Institutional self now coordinates all its relationships, which have been shifted to the object-pole. Interpersonal feelings of mutuality are still important, but not all-important as they once were. They have now been relativized within the new ultimate context of the self-system, which regulates them and incorporates them into its Institutional balance.

Kegan uses Ibsen's *A Doll's House* to illustrate the shift from the Interpersonal self to the Institutional self, from psychological dependence to independence. He points out that Nora is not simply rejecting the ideas of others, nor merely coming to some better ideas of her own. Rather, Nora "is coming to a new set of ideas *about* her ideas, about where ideas even come from, about who authorizes them, or makes them true." As Kegan stresses, "she is making a bid for independence not merely from someone else's ideas but from *anyone* else's ideas from a source external to her that can create and validate her ideas. Her discovery is not just that she herself has different ideas, but that she has been uncritically, unawarely identified with external sources of ideas (her husband, her church, and her culture)." To be uncritically identified with these sources is to be unable to question their ideas. They are taken, says Kegan, as The Truth. Nora is not so much (or even necessarily) rejecting the ideas, values, and beliefs of her husband and pastor as she is rejecting her previous uncritical stance toward them, her being defined by them. Nora's new, emerging independent self is not just a stronger (or more assertive) version of her former dependent self. By relativizing the ideas that had previously defined her, Nora now *has* them as object, and no longer *is* them as subject. This, Kegan emphasizes, "is *a wholly different way of constituting what the self is, how it works, what it is most about*."[34] Nora now explicitly recognizes a duty toward herself, but in fact she had also been dutiful to herself, not just to others, as a "doll wife." Her loyalty has not shifted from others to self; rather, the very realities of other and self are now radically different. Nora is a new self, but she is only at the beginning of a long journey of critical self-creation.

The Institutional self is independent and strong, but its strength is that of the bureaucrat, who is identified with the organization. The very meaning of the Institutional self is derived from its organization. Because this Stage 4 self *is* its organization, there can be no review of the organization's policies. Thus the Institutional self is not only subject to its own policies, but vulnerable to the excesses of control that corrode every unlimited organization. Just as the Interpersonal self's relationships needed to be relativized, so too does the Institutional self's organization; but that must wait. The

Institutional self is not a final goal, then, but it is a self that Mary needs to realize, as difficult as transition to it will be for her.[35]

Before ending our consideration of adolescence and moving on to young adulthood, we should discuss the critical transitional phase between conventional and postconventional morality, the relativist orientation that Kohlberg names Stage $4^1/_2$.

The conventional moral orientation of Stage 4 is the culminating achievement of many years of socialization. But because of the radical freedom and creativity of personal consciousness, socialization cannot be total, and so conventionality is not the last word in moral development. The formal operational thought that makes Stage 4 social moral reasoning possible also grounds the critical questioning that undermines the "taken for granted" absoluteness of conventional morality. In order for formal thinking to become socially subversive, some psychological distance from one's conventional world is necessary. This often happens in our society through the experience of leaving home and moving into college life. This distance gives one the mental "elbow room" for reflective thought to turn back on one's self and one's world and raise critical questions. Of course, college life does not always effect this critical turn, and it is not the only route to it. But the college experience can generate truly critical thinking if one encounters people from other worlds seriously, and if the resulting plurality of values is then mediated by an effective liberalizing and liberating curriculum. That, at least, is the theory; in actuality, all too often college just means four more years of conventional socialization, not a radical critique of it.

In the psychosocial moratorium of identity questioning, radical criticism of one's world can bring about a relativistic breakthrough of the conventional social system's absolute givenness. Kohlberg sees this radical relativism as a necessary condition for development to postconventional principled reasoning; the unquestioned absoluteness of Stage 4 conventional morality must be undermined if moral reasoning is to advance. Until principled moral reasoning emerges, however, relativism reigns, and the validity of morality—identified with the conventional reasoning of Stage 4—is rejected. This Stage $4^1/_2$ relativistic period is ideally a transitional phase to a principled postconventional orientation, but some people never make the move to principled reasoning, and spend the rest of their lives in the moral quicksand of relativism, with no reason to think that one opinion could be better than another. These people understand conventional morality, but, having seen through its alleged absoluteness, can never really go home to it again. In Kohlberg's view, of course, most people are spared this problem because they never advance beyond the apparent safety of conventional morality in the first place. Mary represents another, very particular type of premature (preconventional) moral relativism. Thrown into the countercultural world of a 1960s college campus after her junior year of high school, she suffered in an especially severe way the moral disorientation that afflicted many young people of the time.

THE YOUNG ADULT:
DESIRE FOR INTIMACY,
MUTUALITY, COMMITMENT

Intimacy, Ethical Strength, and Adult Knowing

The psychosocial hallmark of young adulthood is shared identity. In Erikson's life-cycle perspective of sequential crises, young adulthood is characterized by the tension between intimacy and isolation. In this view, "the young adult, emerging from the search for and the insistence on identity, is eager and willing to fuse his identity with that of others." The young adult, Erikson highlights, "is ready for intimacy, that is, the capacity to commit himself to concrete affiliations and partnerships and to develop the ethical strength to abide by such commitments, even though they may call for significant sacrifices and compromises."[36] This intimacy "is really the ability to fuse your identity with somebody else's without fear that you're going to lose something yourself."[37] Later we will distinguish sharply between intimacy and fusion, but here I want to relate the lack of fear of self-loss to identity. Only "consolidated identity permits the self-abandonment demanded by intimate affiliations, by passionate sexual unions, or by inspiring encounters."[38] This relationship between consolidated identity and intimacy clearly illustrates the developmental principle that, in Erikson's words, "the strength acquired at any stage is tested by the necessity to transcend it in such a way that the individual can take chances in the next stage with what was most vulnerably precious in the previous one."[39] Thus identity is tested by intimacy. In order for a young person to have the confident strength to risk reaching out to another in an intimate relationship, he or she must have basically resolved the adolescent crisis of identity. The strength of consolidated identity should not be confused with the popular "strong ego," whose strength is for self-centeredness, not for the self-transcendence of mutual intimacy. Not surprisingly, Erikson identifies the specific virtue of young adulthood as love, "the *mutuality of mates and partners in a shared identity,* for the mutual verification through an experience of finding oneself, as one loses oneself, in another."[40]

We have just seen Erikson refer to "ethical strength" in connection with the intimacy of young adulthood. In fact, what distinguishes adulthood from adolescence, in Erikson's view, is an ethical orientation. As he sees moral development, the moral learning of childhood is succeeded by the ideological experimentation of adolescence, which in turn finally submits to the realistic demands of adult experience, resulting in an ethical orientation. By "ethical" Erikson means "a *universal sense of values assented to* with insight and foresight, in anticipation of immediate responsibilities, not the least of which is a transmission of these values to the next generation."[41]

The "insight" which makes the ethical orientation possible is the realistic understanding characteristic of genuinely adult knowing. With Piaget we have seen that specifically adult knowing is achieved only when formal operations are complemented by concrete experience of the work world. Only then does adolescent egocentrism surrender to realistic judgment. The systematic and reflective power of formal operations remains, but now always in dialectic tension with the conflicting realities of the complex context of concrete social experience. Adult knowing recognizes the relativity of every context, and this relativity brings the totalistic logic of flighty adolescent thought back down to earth. Finally, in its fullness, adult knowing overcomes the idealistic adolescent's demand for certitude with a realistic appreciation of the relativity and probability inherent in the search for genuine understanding. We will see the effects of this specifically adult knowing on moral reasoning and faithing soon, but first we will consider what is happening with the self during this period of young adulthood.

The Interindividual Self:
Postconventional Morality and Faith

We last saw Kegan's self at the Institutional stage, immersed in its own organization at the subject-pole. But with the affective and cognitive developments we have just considered, the self in young adulthood has the strength to transcend its psychic organization by shifting it to the object-pole where the self can now direct and run it. Now the self no longer *is* its organization. This Stage 5 freedom from its psychic institution means that the self can relate to others as fully personal individuals—people, as Kegan says, "who are known ultimately in relation to their actual or potential recognition of themselves and others as value-originating, system-generating, history-making individuals." Now the Interindividual self's "community is for the first time a 'universal' one in that all persons, by virtue of their being persons, are eligible for membership."[42] We will soon see how this quality of the Interindividual self is manifested in the moral and faith dimensions.

From the perspective of the Stage 5 Interindividual self, Kegan makes a fundamental distinction between intimacy and fusion. Erikson's use above of "fusing" in relation to intimacy notwithstanding, Kegan insists on the necessity of distinguishing the quality of interpersonal relationship characteristic of Stage 5 from that of Stage 3. Because at Stage 5 there is a self to be brought to others, truly intimate sharing of distinct identities is possible. In contrast, at Stage 3, where the self *is* its relationships and thus is derived from others, there is no distinct identity to share, only an unformed identity to melt into fusion. And this is precisely Mary's problem as she reaches for an intimacy that she is still developmentally incapable of.

Because the Stage 5 Interindividual self is capable of intimacy with itself—that is, it can recognize and tolerate emotional conflict within itself—it can enjoy genuine intimacy with others. In contrast, at Stage 3 the Interpersonal self does not have the strength to admit emotional conflict within itself, and at Stage 4 the stronger Institutional self, though capable of recognizing internal conflict, sees it as a dangerous element—not to be tolerated but "handled" in the most cost effective manner possible. Freed from subjection to its organization, the self at Stage 5 no longer sees emotional conflict as ultimately dangerous, and openly receives it in interior conversation. By transcending the "counterdependent independence" of Stage 4, the Interindividual self can "give itself up" to another in interdependence, where it finds itself as distinct in what Erikson calls "a counter-pointing of identities."[43]

Unlike the last stage in many developmental models, Kegan's Interindividual self is, by definition, not a closed end of isolated independence. It is open, dynamic, flowing. It is, however, a decisive point in the process of differentiation and integration that began with the creation of self and other in infancy. Unlike other stages which emphasized either differentiation or integration, the Interindividual balance features a distinct self (differentiation) that is brought into being through the very sharing of itself (integration). This stage is a true balance, tipped toward neither differentiation nor integration, because the two great yearnings of the human spirit—for separateness or independence and for attachment or connectedness—now coexist in creative tension within a self defined by their joint existence: relational autonomy.

We left Kohlberg's analysis of moral reasoning development at the transitional phase he calls Stage $4^1/_2$ relativism. There the cognitive power of advanced formal operations allowed reflective thought to turn back critically on the self and its conventional world. The resulting subversion of the taken-for-granted absoluteness of conventional morality's authority is, in Kohlberg's view, a necessary but not sufficient condition for the principled moral reasoning of the postconventional orientation. In order to overcome Stage $4^1/_2$ relativism and move positively toward principled moral reasoning, critical reflective thought must be complemented by the twofold experience of specifically adult responsibility: the experience of making more or less irreversible decisions for one's own life and for the welfare of others. In our society, this usually, but not always, means being financially independent on the one hand, and being a parent on the other. Through such experience is the adolescent's abstract, idealistic thinking transformed into the contextual and dialectical thinking of the realistic adult. We will see the fullness of this adult moral experience in the caring generativity of Erikson's next stage of the life cycle.

Kohlberg understands the normatively adult moral reasoning of the postconventional orientation in terms of autonomous principles that have validity independent of any external authority. The truly autonomous, principled person is her own moral authority, the author of her own moral life. The postconventional social perspective is prior-to-society, with an emphasis on the legal at Stage 5 and on the ethical at Stage 6.

Postconventional moral Stage 5 is characterized by Kohlberg as a social-contract orientation with legal and utilitarian qualities. Here critically examined rights and standards that are commonly agreed upon define right behavior. Procedural rules for reaching agreement help to overcome the perceived relativism of personal values. At this stage laws embodying social morality are subject to change in order to enhance social life, not frozen as at Stage 4. Stage 5 is reflected in the democratic structures of the United States, an important political point considering Kohlberg's judgment that most American adults are at the conventional Stages 3 and 4. We will switch over to the faith development track now, leaving the completion of the postconventional moral orientation to our consideration of middle adulthood.

Just as a radical breakthrough in the development of moral reasoning is required to move from a conventional to a postconventional orientation (specifically, from Stage 4 to Stage 5), so too is an equally radical breakthrough necessary in faith development in order to move from Fowler's Stage 3 Synthetic-Conventional Faith to Stage 4 Individuative-Reflective Faith. And if the moral reasoning transition involves a relativistic moment, the faith transition involves an atheistic moment—the excruciating dark night between the death of one God and the birth of another. At that moment, of course, it is the death that is experienced, while the birth is at best a distant conceptual possibility, if anything. But on the other side of nothingness is a breakthrough to, as Fowler puts it, a new self-awareness and personal responsibility for one's commitments, lifestyle, beliefs, and attitudes. Not even experienced counselors and directors can diminish the pain of losing one's self, one's world, one's God, but they can compassionately accompany a person through the suffering.

Demythologizing is also involved in the transition to the postconventional faith of Stage 4, the translation of multivalent symbols into clearer, more straightforward conceptual meanings. This is the rationalism of one's personal Enlightenment. And Fowler

points out that the young adult who experiences this transition to
Stage 4 is also forced to face certain unavoidable tensions hereto-
fore submerged in a conforming, member-of-society perspective:
individuality vs. belonging to a community, subjectivity vs. objectivity, self-fulfillment vs. service to others, and the relative vs. the
absolute. At Stage 4 these universal tensions are on the table to be
dealt with, but not successfully resolved, as they are usually collapsed into one side or the other. When they arise in a client's life,
such tensions make great demands on the knowledge of counselors and directors. At the point of Mary's conversion, of course,
none of this had yet surfaced in an explicit way.

THE MIDDLE AND OLDER ADULT: THE QUEST FOR INTERIORITY AND FINAL INTEGRATION

Generativity, Universal Ethics, and Paradoxical Faith

The maturity of middle adulthood relates to the seventh crisis of
the life cycle that Erikson specifies as generativity versus stagna-
tion. Here the meaning of generativity includes not only productiv-
ity in the economic sense, but the bringing forth of "everything that
is generated from generation to generation: children, products,
ideas, *and* works of art."[44] But for Erikson generativity is "primarily
the concern with establishing and guiding the next generation."[45]
This is directly connected with Erikson's psychosocial understanding that "adult man is so constituted as to *need to be needed* lest he
suffer the mental deformation of self-absorption, in which he
becomes his own infant and pet."[46] From the successful resolution
of the crisis of generativity emerges the strength of care, "the broad-
ening concern for what has been generated by love, necessity, or
accident—a concern that must consistently overcome the ambivalence adhering to irreversible obligation and the narrowness of
self-concern."[47] Such generative caring, of course, lies at the heart
of the ethical orientation. Indeed, it is precisely this caring that
Carol Gilligan has focused on in her effort to delineate the characteristic moral strength of women. By doing so, she has helped us to
see that the fully human goal of moral development is an integrated

caring justice.[48] To consider the full universality of this orientation, we turn now to Kohlberg's Stage 6.

While an orientation to internal decisions of conscience develops from Kohlberg's Stage 5 contract viewpoint, Stage 5 lacks the comprehensive, universal, and consistent ethical principles that constitute Stage 6, the highest stage of moral reasoning. Stage 6's defining elements are the "universal principles of justice, of the reciprocity and equality of human rights, and of respect for the dignity of human beings as individual persons."[49] Though Stage 6 moral judgments are surely judgments of personal conscience, they are the judgments of a conscience that subjects itself to universal principles. Persons at moral Stage 6 are autonomous in terms of conventional morality, but always rooted in fundamental human values formalized in universal ethical principles. These universal principles are not like the concrete moral rules of Stage 4, approving or disapproving certain kinds of actions (such as, for example, the Ten Commandments), but more like formal, abstract versions of values or ideals (like, for example, the Golden Rule or the categorical imperative). The role of universal ethical principles is not to tell us exactly how to act or not to act, but to serve as a higher ethical court, as a standard against which moral rules can be critically appraised. To take one clear example from social morality in the Western world, the ancient moral rules allowing slavery finally collapsed in the nineteenth century under the critique of the universal ethical principles of justice and the dignity of the human person. With this much said about the highest stage of moral reasoning, we can turn now to the upper reaches of faith development.

At Stage 4 of faith development we saw a breakthrough to new self-awareness and personal responsibility accompanied by the one-sided collapse of universal tensions and the demythologizing of multivalent symbols. The Conjunctive (Paradoxical-Consolidative) Faith of Stage 5 maintains the heightened sense of self, but goes a long way toward overcoming the reductionism of Stage 4. Now the "other" is taken with full seriousness. Thus the (possibly thirty-something) adult at Stage 5 "affirms and lives out its own commitments and beliefs in such a way as to honor that which is true in the lives of others without denying the truth of its own."[50]

Faith Stage 5 is the point at which a person experiences what Paul Ricoeur has named the "second naiveté," the post-critical retrieval of the dynamic symbol lost in the personal Enlightenment of Stage 4's interest in clarity and certainty. This recognition of the symbolic as real is best understood as a quality of genuinely critical knowing. At Stage 5 the critical self no longer qualifies the symbolic with a "merely." As part of its openness to the other, the self is now ready to encounter the personal and social unconscious, with all its mysterious and powerful riches. This radical openness and symbolic power of Stage 5 support the generative adult in its commitment to universal ethical principles, a commitment that includes full awareness of the cost.

Integrity and Universalizing Faith

Carl Jung has pointed out that in the second half of life we are called in a special way to enter our interiority, and there to explore questions about the ultimate meaning of life, questions that are essentially religious.[51] Similarly, in the advanced years of adulthood Erikson specifies the last of the life-cycle crises, integrity vs. despair. "In the aging person who has taken care of things and people and has adapted to the triumphs and disappointments of being, by necessity, the originator of others and the generator of things and ideas—only in him the fruit of the seven stages gradually ripens."[52] The strength appropriate to this stage "takes the form of wisdom in its many connotations—ripened 'wits,' accumulated knowledge, inclusive understanding, and mature judgment." The wisdom of integrity loves life in the face of death. As despair is the natural result of a self-centered life, so integrity and wisdom are the natural outcome of a self-transcending life. While meaningful old age can give the indispensable perspective of an integrated heritage to the next generations, the end of the life cycle also raises "ultimate concerns." In this context, Erikson's basic point is that "whatever chance man has to transcend the limitations of his self seems to depend on his full (if not tragic) engagement in the one and only life cycle permitted to him in the sequence of generations."[53] Having raised this fundamental religious question, we will now follow it up in the perspectives of Kohlberg and Fowler.

The fact that the moral heroes Kohlberg cites as models of Stage 6—Martin Luther King, for example—were also deeply religious led him to reflect on "the relation of the development of religious faith to the development of moral principles."[54] In Kohlberg's under-standing of the moral stages, even Stage 6 provides only an imper-fect resolution to the problem of life's meaning, what Kohlberg takes to be the essence of Erikson's crisis of integrity vs. despair. Even for someone with an awareness of the universal principles of justice, there still remains the fundamental issue of justifying jus-tice: "Why be just in a universe full of injustice?" While this ques-tion can be raised at any moral stage, Kohlberg thinks that it "cannot arise on a psychologically serious level until a man has attained moral principles and lived a life in terms of these princi-ples for a considerable length of time."[55] Though Stage 6 may over-come the skeptical doubts of moral relativism, even universal ethical principles cannot overcome the radical doubt of "Why be moral at all?" And this question entails the most profound existen-tial questions like "Why live?" or "How face death?" In other words, ultimate moral maturity requires answers to questions that are not really moral but religious.

In Kohlberg's assessment, these questions cannot be answered on purely rational grounds, but he does think there are meaningful solutions to religious questions that are "compatible with rational science and principled ethics." He employs a metaphorical Stage 7 to point toward these religious solutions. Whether God language is used or not, Stage 7 solutions involve nonegoistic or nondualistic contemplative experience. As Kohlberg understands it, the essence of this experience is "the sense of being a part of the whole of life and the adoption of a cosmic as opposed to a universal humanistic (Stage 6) perspective." After an initial phase of despair, this Stage 7 cosmic perspective becomes a state of mind in which "we identify ourselves with the cosmic or infinite perspective, itself; we value life from its standpoint."[56] This perspective brings us to Fowler's high-est faith stage.

Fowler's Stage 6 Universalizing Faith goes beyond Stage 5's para-doxical balancing of "opposites" by transcending all dichotomies in an identification with all Being, including the transcendent, in a community of universal inclusiveness. At Stage 6 one "becomes a disciplined, activist incarnation of the imperatives of absolute love and justice...."[57] Thus the paradox of being-for-others disappears. At Stage 6 one is being most truly oneself in being for others. Full self-actualization is realized in full self-transcendence. Here, therefore, too, is the most profound self-love, now identified with neighbor-love. In sum, across the personal spectrum—from the cognitive and affective dimensions to the moral and faith dimensions—development of the self occurs through self-transcendence: self-realization is self-transcendence. In the next chapter we will consider the crucial points in this developing realization of self-transcendence called conversions.

Chapter 7

The Self in Radical Transformation: Spiritual Direction for Christian Conversion

A central thesis of this study of the desiring self is that self-transcendence, properly understood, is the criterion of both authentic self-realization and the gospel's call to loving service of the neighbor. As such, self-transcendence is the goal of both pastoral counseling and spiritual direction. Although pastoral counseling and spiritual direction, as we saw in Clinebell's "Revised Model," are not separate realities in practice, they can be distinguished in terms of development and conversion. Pastoral counseling, as we have seen, seeks to promote self-transcendence by facilitating personal development, especially when development faces serious obstacles. If pastoral counseling deals with specific developmental and other problems in a client's life, spiritual direction can be said to address the very meaning of the client's life itself, to address the realization of the self's most radical desire, of its fullest, divine potential. Spiritual direction, in other words, aims at realizing the self-transcending possibilities of a client's life by encouraging radical transformation of the self within its ongoing development, by encouraging, in a word, conversion.[1] As an aid in discerning such conversions, or their possibilities, in clients like Mary, for example, this chapter will suggest developmental guidelines for explicating the biblical meaning of conversion as a call to the fullness of life.

In the Judeo-Christian tradition, conversion has first and foremost meant a turning, redirection, change of heart, renewal. It was no accident that John the Baptist preached repentance for sin. He was, after all, in that long line of Hebrew prophets who called their people to turn from sin to God. And after John's arrest, Jesus continued the call to conversion as he proclaimed the good news of God in Galilee: "This is the time of fulfillment. The reign of God is at hand! Reform your lives and believe in the gospel!" (Mk 1:15)

From the beginning, then, conversion has meant return—return to God from sinful ways. And so it has been throughout Christian history as the community of God's people has been blessed with special moments of renewal, with individual and corporate transformations of life, some particularly striking—one thinks of Augustine and Monica, Francis and Clare, Ignatius and Teresa—most rather ordinary, but all of them important steps on the return to God's ways. The phrase, "return to God's ways," suggests a journey, and that is how many Christians today experience conversion: a long, day after day, year after year struggle through rough desert terrain, but inspired by the joyful goal of a "promised land" of love and justice, and supported by the caring hand of God's presence.

Like many other personal and experiential realities, however, conversion has not always had a prominent place in institutionalized Christianity. At different periods, including the twentieth century, it even seems to have been "lost" for a time. In recent decades, however, conversion has been rediscovered by Christians. It has even become fashionable—from the White House, to Wall Street, to the NFL. This should be good news. The problem from a spiritual direction perspective, however, is that, in its popularity, conversion can mean just about anything anyone wants it to mean. Not all "conversions" are authentically Christian. And, if we needed convincing, this fact was brought home to us rather rudely not too many years ago when the Christian sideshow of TV evangelism exposed its seamy underbelly to the world—a phenomenon that journalists like Ted Koppel found irresistibly fascinating.

So, if conversion really is fundamental to Christian life, spiritual directors must ask some tough, critical questions about the nature of this personal reality that is the key to a life of self-transcendence. They need to establish criteria for discerning authentic from inauthentic conversions. A good place to start is with William James, who really defined the rules of the modern conversion game at the turn of the century in his classic *Varieties of Religious Experience*. James saw conversion as a psychological process of unification of a divided self. In his interpretation, conversion is primarily a phenomenon of adolescence or youth, responding to what Erik Erikson would later call an identity crisis. And, for James, conversion is not essentially religious, since religion is only one of the many forms the psychological process of unification may take.[2] When this essentially psychological process occurs in an explicitly religious context, like nineteenth-century Protestant revivalism, it may assume the language, images, and color of religion, but this does not make it a radically religious experience.

None of this is meant to discredit James's valuable interpretation, but merely to identify it as primarily focused on the psychological and the adolescent. Indeed, the value of James's approach continues, with more systematic precision, in Erikson's psychosocial theory of development. But Erikson not only locates James's understanding of conversion in the identity crisis of adolescence or youth, he also relativizes it within a larger lifespan context, a context that suggests a more complex, differentiated understanding of conversion, including the possibility of a truly radical religious dimension. From the Eriksonian perspective, the last four crises of the life cycle (identity, intimacy, generativity, and integrity) may all be regarded as opportunities for fundamental conversions.

At this point, in order to keep the discussion as concrete as possible, I will introduce a real life example of conversion in the person of Thomas Merton, the young convert to Roman Catholicism who lived his adult life as a Trappist monk and died in Bangkok pursuing contemplative dialogue with Buddhist monks. We have already considered Merton's understanding of the true self; now we will look at key points in his life experience. Merton is a particularly good example in this context of pastoral counseling and spiritual direction because he not only experienced conversion himself, and wrote about it perceptively, but he also had an acute interest in psychotherapy. Indeed, he wrote about both conversion and psychotherapy in terms of self-transcendence. Sharing this study's basic presuppositions, Merton saw a self-transcending realization as the only fully authentic realization of the human person's potential. He wrote about this full self-transcendence—in contrast to the social adjustment of the false self—as a "final integration" of the true self, a state of transcultural maturity. For Merton, the "fully born" person "apprehends his life fully and wholly from an inner ground that is at once more universal than the empirical ego and yet entirely his own." Having "attained a deeper, fuller identity than that of his limited ego-self," the finally integrated person is in a way identified with everybody—he is "all things to all men."[3] This is the goal of pastoral counseling and spiritual direction as they seek to liberate the radical personal desire for self-transcendence. In many minds, unfortunately, Merton and conversion have been linked to his youthful conversion to Roman Catholicism.[4] But to focus on the young Merton's conversion is to obscure the deeper religious experience of his mature years, to miss the profound dimensions of conversion available only in adulthood.[5]

Here, employing the work of the developmental theorists we saw in the previous chapter, I will set Bernard Lonergan's multidimensional view of conversion into a lifespan context, and use it to explicate Merton's life as a continuing process of transformation with four distinct, specifiable moments of conversion. In its simplest terms, conversion for Lonergan is an about-face, a radical reorientation of one's life. His analysis specifies cognitive, moral, affective, and religious conversions.[6] In developmental terms, these conversions can be situated, respectively, within the analyses of Piaget on cognition, Kohlberg on moral reasoning, Erikson on psychosocial affectivity, and Fowler on faith. Cognitive conversion is the critical discovery of oneself as a knower. Moral conversion is the choice of value as a criterion for decision. Affective conversion is a falling-in-love which reorients the dynamic thrust of one's life toward others. Religious conversion, like affective, is a falling-in-love that establishes a person as a dynamic principle of benevolence and beneficence. But in religious conversion one falls in love with God, one is grasped by ultimate concern. Being-in-love with God is "total and permanent self-surrender without conditions, qualifications, reservations." Here I shall use cognitive conversion to distinguish between two forms of moral conversion: basic, uncritical moral conversion and critical moral conversion. (The same distinction based on the presence or absence of cognitive conversion also applies to affective and religious conversions.)

This chapter's aim is to expand and enrich our understanding of conversion as a foundational moral-religious reality across the lifespan. Merton's life experience will give concrete shape to the conversion theory, and illustrate its adequacy for the full complexity of the moral-religious life.

The chapter will trace Merton's distinct moments of conversion in chronological order. In successive sections we shall consider (1) Merton's early conversion as a *basic moral* conversion, a new way of living rooted in the virtues of fidelity and justice; (2) his deepening and confirmation of this first conversion in the monastery as an *affective* conversion, a new way of loving grounded in generosity and forgiveness; (3) his taking full cognitive possession of this deepened conversion and expanding it socially and politically as a *critical moral* conversion, a new way of knowing anchored in empathy and humility; and finally (4) his radical relativization of the autonomy of this moral-affective conversion in total surrender as a *religious* conversion, a new way of being secured in the realities of gift and surrender. With Merton, of course, all these conversions are dimensions of a single, ongoing personal story that is fundamentally Christian, though, as we shall see, eventually open to every form of authentic religious experience. Such openness to the other major religious traditions is now indispensable for the Christian spiritual director.

The point of this framework is not to put conversion in a straightjacket by claiming that there are only certain kinds of conversion and that they can only occur at certain moments. The point, rather, is to highlight optimal times in a person's life when some radical conversion possibilities are at their height, thus allowing us to discern them more easily and to support them more effectively. Such a framework will also make it eminently clear that Christian conversion is a lifelong enterprise. Renewal is never complete; each season of life, rather, is an opportunity for a conversion with a particular shape and meaning of its own.

In speaking of Christian conversion, of course, I am not referring only or primarily to the initial process of becoming a Christian, of joining a Christian church, which is certainly a conversion when it marks a significant interior turning in one's life. For conversion also and especially means the interior transformation that may be experienced by a person who is already a Christian, either from birth or through an earlier conversion. So Christian conversion is not just a matter of believing something new, of affirming a new faith, of adopting a new story. Conversion is not just a change of content, a switching over from one faith story to another. But, much more importantly, Christian conversion is the introduction of a new *kind* of story into one's life, a story with its own intrinsic requirements for moral, affective, cognitive, and religious transformation.

Christian conversion demands that one live, love, understand, and even be in a new way. Christians must be morally converted, but moral conversion is not first of all a matter of choosing new values (content), but of choosing value as the criterion of one's choices. Christians must be affectively converted, but affective conversion is not primarily a question of loving someone new (content), but of allowing love to become the central reality, the dynamic principle of one's life. Christians must be cognitively converted, but cognitive conversion is not first of all knowing something new (content), but understanding one's knowing, and thus oneself, in a new way. And Christians must be religiously converted, but religious conversion is not primarily a matter of new forms of prayer and worship (content), but of allowing God to move from the edges to the center of one's life, transforming one's very way of being. Radical Christian conversion, then, is not simply a change of content, but a structural transformation of the self. Now, to see what all this means in concrete Christian experience, we turn to the life of Thomas Merton.

BASIC MORAL CONVERSION: A NEW WAY OF LIVING

Merton's youthful conversion to Roman Catholicism was clearly a Christian conversion with important cognitive, affective, moral, and religious qualities. By stressing here the moral dimension, I do not mean to deny Merton's conversion its multiple qualities or its Christian character. I simply intend to identify it specifically as a Christian *moral* conversion.[7]

Merton's years as a student at Columbia University in the late 1930s constituted a period of sustained development in his moral judgment and decision-making powers. For much of that time he was engaged in an almost singleminded effort to reach a decision— a decision constitutive of his very life, of the kind of person he would be. On his return to the United States from Cambridge University in 1934 he was, at age nineteen, in the middle of an extended period of self-centered licentiousness he had thrown himself into after his father's death three years earlier. Although he had made some commitment to Communism, Merton would look back on this time and judge "that my inspiration to do something good for mankind had been pretty feeble and abstract from the start. I was still interested in doing good for only one person in the world—myself." By 1937 a physical breakdown reflected the inner life of the "big man on campus." "I had done what I intended, and now I found that it was I who was emptied and robbed and gutted. What a strange thing! In filling myself, I had emptied myself."[8]

In Merton's struggle toward conversion and decision for the monastic priesthood, then, we have the young man in what Erikson's psychosocial life cycle names an identity crisis.[9] Erikson's interpretation of identity resolution in terms of a commitment in fidelity to value specifies an intrinsically moral dimension in youthful conversion. This commitment can be seen as the personal, affective correlative to the key transition from preconventional to conventional moral reasoning specified by Kohlberg's structural stage theory.[10]

While Kohlberg gives no attention to conversion, careful reflection on the nature of his structural stages indicates that stage transition (especially between major levels) is a form of conversion. Kohlberg claims that the transition from preconventional to conventional moral reasoning occurs at the earliest in the adolescent, occasioned in part by the emergence of what Piaget calls formal operations.[11] Fundamentally this transition is a shift from a pre-moral to a moral orientation, that is, from a radically egocentric orientation in which the criterion for decision is self-interested satisfaction (Merton at Cambridge and in his early years at Columbia), to a social orientation in which the criterion for decision is value (Merton in his call to Catholicism and the monastery). When structural and psychosocial stages coincide, moral conversion to value meshes perfectly with the adolescent's discovery of self in fidelity. And from this emerges a new sense of justice. Moral conversion's orientation to persons and society gives fairness a new meaning. No longer does fairness mean "getting what I want" (adults know how to translate the ten-year-old's cry, "it's not fair!"—even if we use it occasionally ourselves). Through moral conversion fairness becomes a sense of justice: recognizing one's obligation to respect the rights of everyone.

Merton's conversion was not simply the resolution of an identity crisis clothed in pious Christian language, as so many classic

adolescent conversion accounts seem to be. By 1941 Merton had
not only "developed a conscience" as he put it, he had also committed himself to Christian values in a solidly conventional way
through a basic moral conversion. Merton's self-discovery did not
occur quickly or easily, but when it did come forth, his private mir-
ror of self-satisfied narcissism was shattered and transformed into
the powerful telescope of a moral conversion reaching out to the
universe of value. Still, as personally authentic and life-transforming
as Merton's 1938–1941 Christian conversion was, I am suggesting
that it was essentially a conventional, uncritical conversion to the
given, unquestioned values and beliefs of the Catholic Church. In
the church and the monastery he found the home he had sought
ever since his mother's death when he was six years old.[12]

From the perspective of spiritual direction, it is clear that Christian moral conversion is an ongoing, life-long process, never to be
taken for granted, always in need of attention. A Christian's fidelity
to justice and the other values of Christian life must constantly be
deepened and expanded. This is surely one of the most fundamental and important areas for discernment.

AFFECTIVE CONVERSION:
A NEW WAY OF LOVING

Moral conversion to value calls us to move beyond the self; it is
more a challenge than an achievement; it discloses the gap between
the self we are and self we should be. The challenge to close that
gap is the challenge to move beyond ourselves not only in our
knowing but also in our deciding and our acting—the challenge to
make our action consistent with our judgment of what we should
do and should be. But we only move beyond ourselves with any
regularity insofar as we fall in love. Such falling-in-love enables us
to escape the centripetal force of our persistent egocentric gravity.
Then we become beings-in-love, existential principles of responsible action consistent with our best judgment. The young adult's
Eriksonian crisis of intimacy with its defining strength of love is
one clear occasion for such falling-in-love, a fundamental reloca-
tion of the self's dynamic center of gravity.[13] For this is the time
when, more or less secure in our own identity, we can—even must—

risk that identity by falling in love. We are personally strong in reaching out, in sharing ourselves, not in defensively protecting ourselves in isolation.

Lonergan has suggested that a person is affectively self-transcendent when the isolation of the individual is broken and he or she spontaneously acts not just for self but for others as well. Further, when a person falls in love, his or her love is embodied not just in this or that act or even in any series of acts, but in a dynamic state of being-in-love. Such being-in-love is the concrete first principle from which a person's affective life flows: "one's desires and fears, one's joys and sorrows, one's discernment of values, one's decisions and deeds."[14] This falling-in-love, in other words, is a more or less radical transformation of a person's life: affective conversion. Such conversion turns one's self, shifts one's orientation, from an absorption in one's own interests to concern for the good of others. Just as we can live for the good of a beloved, or of our children, when we count no sacrifice too great, so our love can also extend to the entire human family. Jesus' example of a life in which no one is a stranger can become a reality in us. Affective conversion, then, is the concrete possibility of overcoming moral impotence, of not only being able to make a decision to commit oneself to a course of action or direction of life judged worthwhile or personally appropriate, but of being able to execute that decision over the long haul against serious obstacles.

In sum, affective conversion is a transformation of desire: a turning from desire for possession to desire for generosity. It is a reorientation from the possessiveness rooted in obsessive concern for one's own needs to a self-giving in intimate love of others. Along with the other conversions we are discussing, this transformation of desire lies at the living center of Christian experience. In the shared identity of concern it nourishes in love lies the only possibility of genuine forgiveness.

Merton's deep friendships with students and teachers at Columbia certainly constituted a fundamental element in his conversion and decision for the monastery. Those friendships—and many later ones—remained important as Merton's affective life continued to develop in various ways in the monastery, especially as he began to teach and guide young monks in the 1950s. Perhaps an experience Merton relates from 1958, as he is beginning to appreciate compassion for the world, best represents affective conversion in his journey.

The crucial experience occurred during a visit to Louisville: "At the corner of Fourth and Walnut, in the center of the shopping district, I was suddenly overwhelmed with the realization that I loved all these people, that they were mine and I theirs, that we could not be alien to one another even though we were total strangers." This experience was like waking from a "dream of separateness, of spurious self isolation in a special world, the world of renunciation and supposed holiness." With a sudden clarity, as he watched people go by about their daily lives, Merton saw that although monks are "out of this world" they continue "in the same world as everybody else, the world of the bomb, the world of race hatred, the world of technology, the world of mass media, big business, revolution, and all the rest." Merton ends his published reflections on this discovery with a prayer of gratitude: "Thank God, thank God that I am like other men, that I am only a man among others."[15]

Eight years later Merton would discover just how much he really was a man like other men. In 1966, at the age of fifty-one, Merton fell in love with a nineteen-year-old student nurse who had been assigned to care for him as he was recovering from back surgery just before Easter. Though he agonized for the rest of the year in a struggle between this love and his vows, this experience of loving and being loved seems to have brought Merton's affective conversion to a full and concrete realization. But, as David Cooper points out, what Merton learned about the dichotomy in himself between an ideal self and the actual self came at the cost of what he would describe as the "terrible interior...crisis" and extremely severe anguish that precedes "final integration."[16]

What we have seen about affective conversion makes it obvious, I think, that the encouragement, or nourishment, of such conversion must be at the center of the spiritual direction process. Authentic Christian living demands prayerful reflection on our possibilities for more expansive generosity and ever deeper forgiveness.

CRITICAL MORAL CONVERSION: A NEW WAY OF KNOWING

Cognitive development, which we have seen Piaget trace from the infant's egocentrism to the adult's dialectical realism, is fundamental not only to one's understanding of the world, but also to *self*-understanding. For insofar as a person who has developed through concrete and formal operations to adult realistic judgment can reflect this cognitive power back on the self, precisely as a knower, there is beyond cognitive development also the possibility of cognitive conversion: the critical recognition of the constitutive and normative role of one's own judgment in knowing reality and therefore value. A person who experiences such critical understanding of self as knower ceases to look somewhere "out there" beyond the self for a criterion of the real or the valuable. Cognitive conversion consists precisely in discovering that criterion in the dynamic structure of one's own realistic judgment. Despite appearances, it is precisely because cognitive conversion is rooted in the discovery of one's *reality* as a critical knower that it leads not to arrogance but to humility.

Kohlberg's postconventional level of moral reasoning, rooted in self-chosen, universal ethical principles, requires exactly this kind of cognitive conversion in the moral dimension, that is, critical moral conversion. Basic moral conversion to conventional morality is essentially uncritical, locating authority in absolutely given social values. To become postconventional one must not only relativize conventional values, but one must discover the final criterion of value in one's own critical judgment, and thereby become the author of one's own moral life. Critical moral conversion to a postconventional stance goes beyond restructuring one's horizon in terms of value, then, by grounding that horizon in the reality of oneself as a critical, originating value.[17]

By the late 1950s and early 1960s there was emerging in Merton an awareness of, concern for, and involvement in the social and political dimensions of life, especially the issues of racism and peace.[18] In order to understand this emergence of critical social consciousness, we must recall not only the young Merton's concern about Harlem and the outbreak of World War II before he "left the world" for the monastery,[19] but also his positive reassessment of "the world," his profound transformational experience of 1949-50, the continuing growth of his critical thinking especially as connected with his strained relationship with the Abbot,[20] and his relationship of loving care and responsibility for the scholastics and novices he served as Master.[21] This latter responsibility—Erikson's generativity—was Merton's preparatory school for later social commitment.[22]

It was precisely the kind of adult experience of serious responsibility for others which Kohlberg claims is a *sine qua non* for development to a postconventional moral orientation.[23] Such responsible caring itself requires accurate insight into the realities of ourselves and others.

Caring is the active expression of empathy, the ability to understand and feel with the needs of others, to share and experience their perspectives as vividly as our own. But if empathy, the cognitive root of compassion, is a realistic understanding of others, its "flip side" is humility, a realistic view of ourselves. The ability to become more "subjective" regarding others and more "objective" regarding ourselves is the fruit of cognitive conversion, of taking possession of our critical, realistic understanding. Humility is not pious self-abasement any more than empathy is sentimental pity; both consist of truthful insight into ourselves and others. Both are required for adult, fully human moral lives.

The strong personal security needs that generated Merton's youthful conversion to Roman Catholicism, along with the authority-centered nature of monastic life, had put a drag on the development of his moral reasoning. But Merton's restless spirit would not be tied down, and once he had broken through the monastic walls of conventional morality into the fresh air of critical inquiry, his moral consciousness needed only the fertile ground of existential responsibility for others in order to take root and finally blossom into a postconventional orientation of autonomous conscience. Merton's development was slow, and at times extremely painful, but the roots went deep and laid a sound support system for a conscience of universal ethical principles whose branches would reach to the most important and difficult social-political problems of his day.

The social dimension and principled quality of Merton's mature moral orientation is probably best illustrated by his commitment to the cause of world peace, especially on issues of nuclear warfare. His mature orientation stands in sharp contrast to how the young Merton had dealt with the issue of war back in 1941, just before he entered the monastery. Then, although he had been personally inclined to view killing in war as insupportable on gospel grounds, Merton, the new Catholic convert, made his decision to register for the draft (as a noncombatant objector) on the basis of the church's officially approved just war theory.[24] His moral reasoning then was clearly an advance in commitment over the days of his Communist peace protests, but it was just as clearly conventional, tied to the authority of the ecclesiastical system.

Twenty years later, however, with the United States and the Soviet Union head to head in a nuclear arms race that, after much study and deliberation, he judged to be immoral, Merton took a public, independent stand that directly challenged church as well as government authority. Merton felt that many Christian leaders, in their kneejerk reaction to the threat of atheistic Communism, were as irresponsible in their enthusiastic support of nuclear overkill as were the pragmatic politicians, for whom the moral issue was irrelevant.

There was no doubt about Merton's own response to this call to moral and political authenticity. He became something of a leader within the opposition to the nuclear buildup as he published a stream of articles on the issue. This was not a popular stand to take, especially in the early 1960s, but Merton had to speak out. Even his superiors' attempt to silence him on the topic of peace – the same year as Pope John XXIII's *Pacem in Terris*–had only temporary success; on this issue his voice could not be still. Indeed, before long, this autonomous moral voice would be speaking out as one of the early opponents of the United States' involvement in Vietnam.[25] The high-pitched, untrained moral voice of the young Communist that had changed into that of the conventional young Catholic, and had slowly matured through the years of monastic silence, had in the early 1960s finally found its authentic postconventional pitch, through a critical moral conversion.

Merton's clearly autonomous, principled stance on moral issues, particularly that of peace, leaves no doubt that he had experienced a cognitive conversion leading to the radical appropriation of his own critical power. Moreover, because this critical cognitive conversion was experienced by a contemplative poet in a context that was not only intrinsically moral but fundamentally religious, there was no possibility of its taking the rationalistic shape of absolute autonomy. Merton was a man who breathed the air of divine mystery. He took critical possession of his autonomous mind, but with paradox and contingency in his blood, he was immune to the reductionist illusion of any imperialistic rationalism. Merton's converted intelligence was a critical mind that was in search of and would settle for nothing less than the one true Absolute that is *mystery*.

For many in spiritual direction, Merton's expansion from an uncritical personal piety to the social and political dimensions of Christian moral life may be seen as a normative model. The empathy and humility born of cognitive conversion must be guided to seek the healing of both personal relationships and the structures of society.

RELIGIOUS CONVERSION: A NEW WAY OF BEING

Carl Jung, as we have seen, regarded the second half of life as a special time for interior exploration about the ultimate meaning of life. Commenting on Jung's point, Seward Hiltner asserts that at mid-life, conversion means life or death. After devoting the first half of life to the external affairs of family and livelihood, one must now face the interior depths. The existential clock is ticking. One either reflects at this point, or regresses. Now it is either conversion or the catastrophe of denial and mediocrity.[26]

As we noted in the previous chapter, Kohlberg has speculated about the possibility of a seventh, religious stage following the full development of moral reasoning.[27] He sees such a stage beginning in the despair of perceiving human life as finite from the perspective of the infinite—the meaninglessness of life in the face of death, for example. For him, "Stage 7" points to what he regards as "meaningful solutions" to the question "why live" or "why be moral," that is, questions about the meaning of life. In his view, these questions can be asked in their ultimate religious sense only by the person at Stage 6 who has attempted to live an autonomous, principled life, and inevitably failed. Only such a person can fully appreciate the radical moral impotence, the utter finiteness of human existence.

The essence of nonegoistic or nondualistic contemplative experience involved in these "Stage 7" solutions is, as Kohlberg puts it, "the sense of being a part of the whole of life and the adoption of a cosmic as opposed to a universal humanistic (Stage 6) perspective." The resolution of the initial despair in this cosmic perspective leads to a state of mind in which "we identify ourselves with the cosmic or infinite perspective, itself; we value from its standpoint." Such a state of mind is temporarily achieved even by people who are not "religious" when, on a mountaintop or before the ocean, they sense the unity of the whole and themselves as part of that unity. For Kohlberg, this experience is correlative to Erikson's final psychosocial task of integrating life's meaning.[28]

A key aspect of postcritical faith development in Fowler's theory is the theme of *paradox*.[29] Whereas Fowler identifies the power to reflect critically on one's self and one's world as the characteristic strength of Stage 4 faith, he focuses on ironic imagination as the strength peculiar to Stage 5 Conjunctive Faith. If a person is faithful to experience, the neat boundaries and clear distinctions of the critical, conceptual knowing necessary for the self-certainty of Stage 4 will gradually but inevitably give way to a recovery of the deep, imaginative symbolic life in Stage 5's dialectical-dialogical knowing. If Stage 4's energies were directed toward a clear definition and establishment of self-identity, Stage 5's interests are aimed at the reality beyond the boundaries of that self—both within and without. There emerges at Stage 5, then, not only a radical openness to the truth of others, but a parallel openness to the fuller truth of one's own being. Like Kohlberg's Stage 6 principled moral orientation, Fowler's Stage 5 faith is rooted in the experience of irrevocable commitments and deeds, and, like Kohlberg's "Stage 7," it too knows the sacrament of defeat. Again, like Kohlberg's principled Stage 6, Fowler's Conjunctive Faith of Stage 5 has an apprehension of justice as a universal principle—beyond the limits of class, nation, or religion. But if Stage 5 faith has a transforming vision of reality, it is also painfully aware of the limits of the existing untransformed world. It is, in Merton's phrase, caught in the Belly of a Paradox.

As distinct from affective conversion, religious conversion is specified by Lonergan as "other-worldly falling in love," as "being grasped by ultimate concern," as "total and permanent self-surrender." According to Lonergan, a person's capacity and desire for self-transcendence meets joyful fulfillment when "religious conversion transforms the existential subject into a subject in love, a subject held, grasped, possessed, owned through a total and so an other-worldly love." Beyond all other human loving, "religious loving is without conditions, qualifications, reservations; it is with all one's heart and all one's soul and all one's mind and all one's strength."[30] As such it is the ultimate realization of a multidimensional process of self-transcendence, of moving beyond the self, of reaching out to others.

Religious conversion is not just a process of becoming "religious," but a totally radical reorientation of one's entire life, of one's very self. One turns to God, not to religion, in such a conversion; one allows God to move to the center of one's life, to take over and direct it. Indeed, both persons with, as well as those without, a religious perspective are eligible candidates for a religious conversion in this radical sense. For the former, such an ultimate conversion may be best understood, perhaps, as a conversion from religion to God. When religious conversion is seen from the traditional Christian perspective of self-surrender, the relativization of human autonomy is stressed. Properly understood, one surrenders not oneself or one's personal moral autonomy, but one's deepest (though unadmitted) pretense to absolute autonomy. But such total surrender is rare, and possible only for those who have totally fallen in love with a mysterious, uncomprehended God, for the person who has been grasped by an other-worldly love and completely transformed into a being-in-love. Now one's very being—indeed, all of reality—is seen as gift.[31]

Did Merton experience religious conversion in this radical sense? As personally authentic and life-transforming as Merton's 1938–41 Christian conversion was, I have characterized it as essentially a conventional, uncritical moral conversion to the given, unquestioned values and beliefs of the Catholic Church. I have also suggested that by the end of the 1950s, Merton, through affective and critical conversions, had developed an autonomous, principled moral consciousness rooted in compassion. Significantly, however, Merton understood this moral autonomy to be in no way absolute.[32] He emphasized that what we really seek and need—"love, an authentic identity, a life that has meaning—cannot be had by merely *willing* and by taking steps to procure them."[33]

At Polonnaruwa in Ceylon, during the 1968 Asian journey that was to end in his death, Merton appears to have received this *gift*. As he looked at the giant Buddhas, with "the silence of their extraordinary faces. The great smiles. Huge yet subtle. Filled with every possibility, questioning nothing, knowing everything, rejecting nothing," he was "suddenly, almost forcibly, jerked clean out of the habitual, half-tied vision of things, and an inner clearness, clarity, as if exploding from the rocks themselves, became evident and obvious." In this clarity, Merton realized, "everything is emptiness, and everything is compassion." He did not know when he had ever had "such a sense of beauty and spiritual validity running together in one aesthetic illumination." He wrote: "I don't know what else remains but I have now seen and pierced through the surface and have got beyond the shadow and the disguise."[34]

This description of the Polonnaruwa experience has significant similarities with Merton's understanding of the Zen breakthrough experience of satori. For Merton, as Anne Carr points out, satori is "an inner explosion, a 'bursting open of the inner core of the spirit' which 'blasts the false self to pieces and leaves nothing' but one's inmost or original self."[35] Satori is "a sudden, definitive, integral realization of the nothingness of the exterior self and consequently, the liberation of the real self, the inner 'I'."[36] The real or true self is the Zen no-self. But, in Zen terms, as Carr explains, the real self "finally transcends the distinction between self and not-self."[37] Zen, as Merton understands it, aims at a consciousness "beyond the empirical, reflecting, willing and talking ego," a consciousness "immediately present to itself and not mediated by either conceptual or reflexive or imaginative knowledge."[38]

Zen practitioners may not be particularly interested in moving beyond the pure consciousness of such spiritual experience, but for Merton its special significance is as a "stepping-stone to an awareness of God." Merton could not be more explicit: "If we enter into ourselves, find our true self, and then pass 'beyond' the inner 'I,' we sail forth into the immense darkness in which we confront the 'I AM' of the Almighty."[39] Such transcendent experience is "an experience of metaphysical or mystical self-transcending" as well as "an experience of the 'Transcendent' or the 'Absolute' or 'God' not so much as object but Subject."[40] For Christians there is an infinite gulf between the being of God and the "I" of the inner self, and our awareness of each must be distinguished. Yet, despite this metaphysical distinction, says Merton, in spiritual experience, "paradoxically, our inmost 'I' exists in God and God dwells in it," and in this identity of love and freedom there "appears to be but one Self."[41] The true self is indeed conscious, but it is aware of itself "as a self-to-be-dissolved in self-giving, in love, in 'letting-go,' in ecstasy, in God...."[42]

In such transcendent experience, according to Merton, there is a "radical and revolutionary change in the subject." This radical change in the subject is a "kenotic transformation, an emptying of all the contents of the ego-consciousness to become a void in which the light of God or the glory of God, the full radiation of the infinite reality of His Being and Love are manifested." Understood in the Pauline sense of a participation in "the mind of Christ," this "dynamic of emptying and of transcendence accurately defines the transformation of the Christian consciousness in Christ."[43] Although there are clear similarities between the kenotic self-emptying of Christianity and the Zen Buddhist experience of emptiness, George Kilcourse has emphasized how Merton saw the Christian theological orientation as affective and personal, and the Zen ontological approach as intellectual and existential.[44]

This kenotic participation in "the mind of Christ" is the Christian version of religious conversion, the orientation toward transcendent mystery that climaxes one's radical desire for self-transcendence. This culmination of the self-transcending process is an orientation toward mystery because, although conscious, it is not objectified. In mediating a return to immediacy, as Lonergan expresses it, the contemplative subject has withdrawn from objectification to a prayerful cloud of unknowing.[45] Still, though other-worldly, such radically religious experience must not be understood in any isolated, individualistic sense. Merton was clear on the this-worldly conditions for passage through the deepest recesses of interiority into the world of the sacred: "A man cannot enter into the deepest center of himself and pass through that center into God, unless he is able to pass entirely out of himself and empty himself and give himself to other people in the purity of a selfless love."[46]

In his own life, the mature Merton's commitment to others was constitutive of his very person. Not only in the social arena of global peace and justice, but also in the more personal dimension of life, Merton was on intimate terms with a selfless love's pain of frustration and defeat. Despite this pain, however, his dynamic openness to reality would not be denied. In one direction the Catholic monk moved out to the world of Protestant theology, to the secular world of the civil rights and peace movements, and, of course, to the world of the East. He was convinced that this movement toward the world in all its richness, complexity, but also evil was a necessary condition for moving beyond the self in another direction—toward the depths of the inner self, the true person, and finally the reality of God. This inner movement is a long, arduous journey, for which, Merton gradually learned, one must travel light, jettisoning the nonessentials, if one is to survive the rigors of the desert.

On this inner journey the illusions of absolute autonomy that make the false self's life comfortable become luxuries that make the death of the true self certain. One clings to such autonomy at the cost of authentic life, of the true self. This is the paradoxical truth that is perceived only by what Fowler calls the ironic imagination. There is no doubt that Merton the poet always had a special "feel" for the symbolic, but it was only when that "feel" was freed to explore the darkness of the inner life that Merton came face to face with paradox—not just the paradox of being a contemplative monk with a Madison Avenue schedule, but the radical paradox he discovered at the center of his being: only in losing your self can you find your self.[47] Not without reason does Merton write so persuasively about the existential dread, the dark night that accompanies the loss, the abandonment, indeed, the death of the false self.[48]

For Merton, of course, to find the true self in the center of one's being is also to truly discover God—immediately, concretely, experientially. Merton writes of the *point vierge,* "the virginal point of pure nothingness," where, "in apparent despair, one meets God—and is found completely" at this "center of all other loves."[49] In Christian terms this transcendent experience at the depths of one's subjectivity appears to condition the movement from Fowler's paradoxical Stage 5 Conjunctive Faith to Stage 6 Universalizing Faith. For the rare person of Stage 6 faith, such transcendent experience grounds the felt sense of ultimate environment that is inclusive of all being. As mentioned above, Merton writes of a "final integration," a state of transcultural maturity, in which one is a fully comprehensive self, with a universal, cosmic perspective, identified with everyone, and thus a peacemaker. Such, for Merton, is holiness.

In promoting and supporting one's active search for value, love, and truth, spiritual direction prepares one for the graced discovery of the true self and God at the center of one's being. Each new discernment of life as gift, each small movement toward surrender of self-interest, readies one for such holiness, for the transcendent experience of surrendering totally to absolute Gift. Such, ultimately, is the goal of spiritual direction.

Conclusion

Christian conversion is the concrete form a person's fundamental reorientation to value, love, truth, and God takes when it is shaped by the Christian story. I have distinguished moral, affective, critical, and religious dimensions of Christian conversion at crucial points of transition in the developmental pattern, and engaged them in the explication of Merton's life-long journey. In claiming a normative character for this interpretation, I defined fully religious Christian conversion as a specifically adult reality, while recognizing the developmental possibility of a basic Christian moral conversion in the resolution of the youthful identity crisis. This structural-developmental interpretation resists the conversion claim based only on manifest content change—however emotionally charged or forcefully expressed it may be.

The personal measure of Christian living, therefore, is the conscience that has experienced a Christian conversion at once moral, affective, critical, and religious. Only a person thus converted is fully and concretely sensitive to the loving life of Jesus. In Merton's life we discovered again the fundamental gospel truth that lies at the heart of the Christian tradition: the radical religious conversion of Christian conscience finds its fullest realization in loving compassion—the self-transcending perfection of human care and justice. In its total surrender such religious conversion radically relativizes the moral autonomy of Christian conscience.

In turning life and love upside down, however, religious conversion does not destroy the authentic moral autonomy of personal responsibility. Indeed, the criterion of both religious conversion and the development of personal autonomy is self-transcendence. Justice, generativity, and universalizing faith all insist on mutuality as the norm of authentic autonomy. Only the inauthentic notions of absolute autonomy and self-fulfillment are contradicted by the self-transcending love and surrender of religious conversion. Christian religious conversion is not the antithesis but the completion of personal development toward self-transcending autonomy.[50] While all counseling and therapy should have self-transcending autonomy as their goal, pastoral counseling proceeds explicitly in the context of religious self-transcendence, and spiritual direction aims at the fullness of cognitive, affective, moral, and religious self-transcendence in Christian conversion, at the radical transformation of the self.[51] We will pursue this distinctiveness in the following chapter as we focus again on Mary.

Chapter 8

Mary Revisited

PSYCHOLOGY, THEOLOGY, AND PASTORAL STRATEGY

In Chapter 1 we saw two radically different interpretations of Mary's development and conversion. Fowler specified Mary's development and conversion in terms of Stage 3, Synthetic-Conventional faith. Ford-Grabowsky, critical of Fowler's approach as ego-oriented, internally contradictory, and merely psychological, interpreted Mary's conversion experience in terms of the Jungian self and the Pauline "inner person" or Christian self of Hildegard. In Ford-Grabowsky's view, Mary had two conversions, one from ego to Jung's self, and one from self to Hildegard's Christian self. In this view, Mary exemplified growth in authentic Christian faith, the "inner person" alive in Christ, realities beyond the scope of Fowler's ego psychology, which can only reduce Mary's experience to a case of arrested development.

These two interpretations are rooted in radically different understandings of the relationship between psychology and theology, or, from another angle in traditional language, between nature and grace. Ford-Grabowsky's view assumes that nature and grace are totally separate realms that have little or no interrelationship. Psychology and theology, therefore, deal with separate, unrelated realities: psychology with the natural ego, theology with the graced Christian self of faith. In contrast to this separatist view, Fowler's interpretation assumes a more integrationist view—that nature and grace are intimately bound together, with grace working on and within nature. In short, it assumes a graced nature. Psychology and theology, therefore, are likewise intimately connected, working together in an integrated way.

These two interpretations also lead to two very different pastoral strategies. For Ford-Grabowsky, Mary's faith and character exemplified the authentic Christian self. Her life in Christ, therefore, merely needed the normal, ongoing spiritual sustenance. Faith appears to be understood as univocal, unrelated to and independent from psychological development. If Mary had need of counseling or even therapy, that was related to an ego problem, not to the faith of her Christian self. For Fowler, of course, faith has many faces, some of the most important ones being the six that are delineated as stages in his developmental theory. Faith may be divine, but it is also human, and as such is intimately bound up with the concreteness of the human person. As the old scholastic dictum puts it, "Whatever you take, you mark with your self" (Quidquid recipitur, recipitur secundum modum recipientis). To say that Mary's conversion occurred at faith Stage 3 means, for Fowler, that Mary's Christian faith, not just her ego, was still a good distance from maturity. Pastoral care for Mary, therefore, required a strategy that would help her to overcome the obstacles to her continuing development—the development, that is, of her whole, integrated self in all its dimensions, cognitive, affective, moral, and faith.

In Fowler's faith-development perspective, Mary needed *sponsorship*—the appropriate "affirmation, encouragement, guidance and models for [her] ongoing growth and development." A sponsor or sponsoring community provides trustworthy support and, when necessary, even confrontation. Appropriate sponsorship for Mary would have involved experiences of community worship and education as well as spiritual direction and psychotherapy. All of this might have deepened and expanded the initial commitments of her conversion experience, and "accelerated her movement to a new and more individuated stage of faith."[1]

Mary did receive sponsorship from the Christian communities in which she lived after her conversion. But the sponsorship of these communities assumed that Mary could simply erase the experience of her personal history and start her new Christian life "from scratch." Fowler agrees that Mary needed a decisive break from her preconversion life. But Mary's painful experience after her conversion indicates that preconversion images, habits, and attachments cannot simply be cut off and ignored. Images of the new Christian master story need to be highlighted, but any attempt to bury the preconversion past is to harbor an "internal saboteur." As Fowler explains it, "The series of negations and separations in Mary's earlier life that left her with a strong substratum of mistrust and self-doubt, on the one hand, and gave rise to her willful, stubborn insistence upon autonomy on the other could not simply be obliterated and left behind." Moreover, adds Fowler, "Mary's intelligence and potential for critical reflection could not simply be subordinated to authoritarian external control if there was to be the possibility for constructive growth in her new faith."[2]

Fowler suggests that Mary, after a period of separation from her preconversion life, needed the kind of pastoral and therapeutic care that would assist her in *recapitulating* earlier stages of development. "Through a skillful combination of therapy and the use of forms of prayer and spiritual direction involving guided meditations, Mary might have been helped to rework images of God, self and others formed in infancy and childhood in the light of her new relation to Christ."[3]

"Recapitulation" is Fowler's structural-developmental version of what ego psychologists call "regression in the service of the ego."[4] It is a process of moving back from the point of something like a conversion experience in order to rework and reground the structural strengths of earlier stages in light of one's new center of value, images of power, and decisive master story.[5] While everyone who experiences a conversion will need such spiritual regrounding, it is clear that Mary also needed coordinated therapeutic reworking of earlier stages, especially in terms of trust and autonomy.

The house church communities Mary lived in after her conversion had a very different understanding of how to support a new convert. Rather than recapitulation and transformation, they thought of negation and obliteration. For them, Mary's new being in Christ required a renunciation of her willful self, a separation from everyone and everything in her past, including her past self, as hopelessly fallen and sinful.[6] Because of the pain in one's preconversion life, this cancellation of the past can seem quite attractive to the convert. Interpreted in satanic terms, the past can be very frightening; to acknowledge that this past continues to exist in the new self is too threatening. It is much easier to believe that submission to Christ has destroyed the evil powers of one's past. But, in Fowler's view, as welcome as the obliteration of the past may be, this strategy short-circuits the conversion process, and continues the pain.

The heart of the matter, as Fowler sees it, is this: "Mary's conversion, genuine and powerful though it was, was seriously affected by the failure of the communities in which she found fellowship to sponsor her in the *transformation,* rather than the *negation,* of the willful self." And, as Fowler continues, we can hear the echo of Robert Kegan: "There is a terrible kind of cruelty, no matter how well intended, in demanding the denial of self when there is no selfhood to deny." At best, Mary's self was in pieces. To demand the renunciation of her willfulness was to require her to deny one of the few strengths she had, leaving her with a passive fragment of a self dangerously dependent, as Fowler says, on external authority and internal impulses. Without an integrated self, a new convert will almost inevitably see in such authority and impulses the "workings of the Lord." It is sad, says Fowler, that Mary did not find a community that focused on Christ's promise to bring life abundantly, a community that could have supported her in the development of an individuated identity, with Christ as the "decisive other."[7]

In Fowler's view, Mary's conversion will not be completed until she goes back and dwells again in the key stages of personal faith development—from infancy through later childhood—where trust can be regrounded and primal images and stories reshaped. Such a process of refounding faith and integrating identity would prepare Mary for the intimacy and ministry she seeks. But intimacy and ministry, writes Fowler, again echoing Kegan, "would then be ways of expressing and sharing the personhood [self] Mary is, rather than being the means by which she tried to find and confirm identity [self]."[8]

THE SELF: FOWLER AND FORD-GRABOWSKY

How can our consideration of the self in its development and conversions help us to understand and overcome the major difference between Fowler and Ford-Grabowsky in their interpretations

of Mary? First we should briefly review the understanding of the
self constructed in Chapter 3.

The main point to be emphasized is that the self is one—a complex unity, in tension to be sure, but a unity. We must not allow all
the references to many different "selves" to obscure this fundamental point. We must also remind ourselves about the danger of reification—of making a "thing" of the self or of such other psychic
realities as, for example, the ego.

In my understanding, the self is one: a dynamic, developing,
dipolar, embodied reality constituted by two dialectically related
poles, subjective ("I") and objective ("me"), and radically oriented
beyond itself to the other. William James and others have taught us
how complex and multidimensional the self-as-object is, but it is
always—to a greater or lesser degree—me. Although the self-as-
object realizes the complexity and diversity of the self, it is always
dialectically related to the self-as-subject, the unifying "I." At the
same time, the self-as-subject, the "I," is no pure, isolated "thing,"
but a dimension of the self and, through its dialectical relationship
to the self-as-object, is radically shaped and textured by the experiences of the self. The self is one. Though dipolar, the self is a unity.
In the context of this understanding of the self we can now consider the views of Fowler and Ford-Grabowsky.

As we saw in Chapter 1, Ford-Grabowsky borrows notions of the
self from Jung and from Hildegard of Bingen. She sets Jung's self
and Hildegard's Christian self off against what she calls Fowler's
ego, which she conceives along Jungian lines: the conscious center
of the psychic structure. We will come to Fowler shortly, but we
should note here that Fowler does not explicate his understanding
of the self in Jungian terms and does not systematically characterize it as "ego."

Whatever the merit of Jung's view of the self and of Hildegard's
view of the Christian self, we should be clear that they are hypothetical concepts, not empirical realities.[9] Neither Jung's psychological self nor Hildegard's theological Christian self is
experienced; both are postulated. Moreover, whatever their individual merits, serious questions arise when these two selves—the one
psychological, the other theological—are mixed together in one
conception of the person. Ford-Grabowsky characterizes ego, self,
and Christian self as "levels" of personality; in fact, however, she

often refers to them as if they are separate, even competing, entities. These terms, indeed, are often used in a moral-religious rather than a structural way. For example, Ford-Grabowsky writes about "the difference between the ego-centered person and the God-centered person." Her point is that "When the ego dominates the psyche, one's horizons expand no further than personal concerns, awareness of God being virtually impossible: one can not be conscious of self and God simultaneously." Such a statement makes clear, I trust, how important was our reflection on consciousness in Chapter 3, where we distinguished between consciousness (a subject's presence to itself) and intentionality (the presence of an object to a subject). She continues: "When the self emerges, however, dislodging the petty ego from its place of psychic centrality to the periphery of the psyche, then egotism can begin to be overcome, and awareness of God become possible."[10]

Ford-Grabowsky's critique that Fowler mixes the logically incompatible ego (Stages 1-4) and self (Stages 5-6) into one developmental sequence makes sense only if the ego and self are conceived as two separate entities on different developmental tracks.[11] The same is true of Ford-Grabowsky's deliberately impossible suggestion that Fowler might add a seventh stage to accommodate his theory to the Christian self. The idea of the logical impossibility of a person being simultaneously at two or three stages, as Ford-Grabowsky charges against Fowler, rests entirely on the conception of ego and selves as multiple, separate entities. But this confusion is not found in Fowler. It is Ford-Grabowsky who assigns her own view of ego to Fowler. And it is she who imports the conception of self and Christian self as separate from and in competition with the ego. These Jungian and Hildegardian conceptions are foreign to Fowler, who usually makes only general, unsystematic references to the self.

At the few points where Fowler does discuss the self explicitly, he articulates a view compatible with the understanding of self presented here in Chapter 3. Most recently, he has stated that by *selfhood* he means "the evolving subjective experience of becoming and being a person in relation." For Fowler, we are "indelibly social selves." Only by emerging from the deep social experience of being in the womb and entering a new kind of relatedness do we begin the journey to selfhood. "Eventually, through maturation and continuing interaction with others," he explains, "we attain *selfhood:* we become *reflective selves*–persons in relation."[12]

Earlier, Fowler had explained that his theory of development "presumes a self that is involved in a simultaneous process of *centering* and *de-centering.*" This is a version of the dipolar development discussed in Chapter 6: in one interactional process there are created an ever more fully realized personal self *and* an ever wider and more complex world of the self. At the subject-pole, Fowler sees "an increasingly *individuating* self–a self that as it develops, differentiates itself from a nurturing ethos and gradually, stage by stage, assumes the burden of construing and maintaining for the self a vision of reality, and of taking autonomous moral responsibility within it." In other words, as Fowler understands it, "this process describes an increasingly centered self–a self with boundaries established by increasingly self-chosen, self-aware investments of trust and loyalty."[13]

At the same time as this centering is proceeding, there is at the object-pole a "gradual decentering in the sense that at each stage a more inclusive account is taken of persons, groups, experiences and world views other than one's own. Increasing with each stage," according to Fowler, "there is an effort to find and maintain a mutuality or complementarity with a widened cosmos of being and value."[14] In short, as one becomes more oneself, one's world becomes larger and richer. Authentic subjectivity and genuine objectivity are two sides of the same developmental coin. This single, experienced self–developing through a process of centering and decentering–is Fowler's faithing person, not Jung's ego or self nor Hildegard's Christian self.

From the perspective of the self constructed in this study, neither Fowler's view of the self nor Ford-Grabowsky's is adequate. Ford-Grabowsky's separatist approach and her reliance on Jung and Hildegard result in an understanding of self that is hypothetical and multiple rather than experiential and single. Though commendable for its attempt to take the Christian spiritual life seriously, this view ends up with a separate Christian self that is merely added on to the Jungian understanding of ego and self.

Fowler's understanding is preferable insofar as it is at least implicitly single and experiential, but it is for the most part simply a taken-for-granted common-sense understanding that deals with none of the theoretical issues of the self, such as consciousness, for example, in any explicit way. And, as we have just seen, when Fowler does consider the self explicitly, his common-sense language of simultaneous centering and decentering turns a paradoxical reality of the self into a literal contradiction. So, while the major thrust of Fowler's view of the self is basically compatible with this study's understanding, his self is left too much as a merely background "given" to be truly useful. The valid concerns of both Ford-Grabowsky and Fowler, I suggest, are dealt with in a much more satisfactory manner by this study's explicit, integrated view of the dialectical, desiring self that is realized in its very interaction with the other: persons, world, God.

MARY: DEVELOPMENT AND CONVERSION

The understanding of the self we constructed in Chapter 3, and have just reviewed above, is, of course, a developmental understanding, as explicated in Chapter 6. The dialectic of subject-pole and object-pole that is constitutive of the self works itself out historically in the interactional lives of concrete persons. No two selves, therefore, are the same; but there are, as we have seen, broad patterns of similarity that developmental psychologists have traced through various dimensions of the self—from the initial differentiation of subject-pole and object-pole in infancy through their increasing dialectical complexity in childhood, adolescence, and adulthood.

As a developmental theorist influenced by the Piagetian cognitive-structuralist approach, as well as by Eriksonian psychosocial concerns, Fowler has a mostly implicit understanding of the self that is, of course, radically developmental. As we saw in the previous section, he "presumes" a self in the *process* of centering and decentering. From that perspective, the present study is an attempt to construct the developmental theory of self that Fowler presumes.

Fowler's interpretation of Mary therefore is, as we have seen, a fundamentally developmental interpretation. For the reasons specified in Chapter 1, Fowler saw Mary in terms of Stage 3 Synthetic-Conventional faith, struggling to achieve a positive identity. From Fowler's perspective, faithing is a constitutive dimension of the self; it contributes to making the self what it is. Distinct but not separate, faith and self develop hand in hand. In other words, for Fowler, the single faithing self is the subject of change, of development. Through all the stages of faith and ages of the psychosocial life cycle, there is a single, dynamic self that develops. Now at Stage 3, now at Stage 4, now struggling primarily with identity issues, now with intimacy, but always the one self, the same but different; that is the nature of change. Change requires a subject that changes; development requires a self that develops. Mary is Mary. The college dropout who hit rock bottom is the same Mary who listened to records in her bedroom as a little girl, but different.

Fowler's theory of faith development, Erikson's psychosocial life cycle, and the other developmental theories attempt to explain the dynamics of the change that makes the difference. Much of sameness and difference can be known by the external observer; one can say something like: "She's changed a lot, but she's the same Mary I knew ten years ago." But when we are discussing change in the self, the focus is primarily on the first person singular. In one of her interviews, Mary could tell Fowler about herself as an early adolescent: "I just couldn't seem to find any friends who had similar interests to mine, and I became really withdrawn, and my mother really got onto me about that because she wanted me to be outgoing and have a lively social life and everything, for my own sake. I just couldn't be the way she wanted me to be. I got very withdrawn, and I read. I'd just close myself in my room and read or listen to classical music."[15] Clearly, Fowler not only takes change seriously, but is able to provide an explanatory context for it.

In Chapter 1 we saw Fowler's specification of his reasons for locating Mary at Stage 3 of faith development. Across the range of Fowler's analytic categories—Locus of Authority, Form of World Coherence, Bounds of Social Awareness, Symbolic Function, Form of Logic, Perspective Taking, and Moral Judgment—a consistent pattern of faith appeared: a pattern characterized essentially by an uncritical interpersonal dependence. I find Fowler's analysis of Mary's development thoroughly persuasive. Rather than rehearse it again here, I intend to complement it by considering Mary in light of Kegan's developmental model of the self.

As we saw in Chapter 6, Kegan's understanding of the self unfolds in five stages: Impulsive, Imperial, Interpersonal, Institutional, and Interindividual. Although the self that moves through the stages is more important than the stages themselves, it can be instructive to examine a person in terms of a particular stage's characteristics. Following upon the concrete limitations of the Impulsive and Imperial selves of childhood, the cognitive transformation of adolescence makes possible the mutual and empathic Interpersonal self, characterized by shared feelings. The fact that the cognitive transformation of interpersonal relations makes the Interpersonal self first possible in adolescence does not mean that it is strictly an adolescent reality. The Interpersonal self is, in fact, lived and experienced by many adults, younger and older. That Mary as a young adult is at the Interpersonal stage is not exceptional. That her struggle, influenced by a context of cultural rebellion and highlighted by a conversion experience, is so intensely painful, perhaps is exceptional.

Mary's great need of others is clearly demonstrated in her desperate searching for a community and a husband. She needs them to be a self. To a great degree, Mary *is* her interpersonal relations. When she loses them, she loses her self. How can a person lose her self? Such an idea only makes sense when we recall Lonergan's distinction between the self-as-subject and the self-as-object, and James' understanding of the various dimensions of the "me" or self-as-object. Destruction of the self-as-object can be experienced by the self-as-subject. Listen again to James reflecting on the "social me." For the person who falls in love, says James, the social self is susceptible to the heights of elation and the depths of dejection. "To his own consciousness he is not, so long as this particular social self fails to get recognition...."[16] Self is a reality of consciousness. As realities of consciousness, the most important thing about the self's relationships is what they *feel* like, and the loss of a significant relationship *feels* like death. To transpose a famous line, a person may die only once, but a self can die a thousand times!

Mary's Interpersonal self dies, *is* not, each time her interpersonal relations cease to exist. Mary first risked and lost a good community experience over her obsession with the man she felt God meant her to marry. Following that loss, Mary next drifted away from involvement in another community and its ministry when she threw herself into a relationship—and quickly marriage—with Harry. After that extremely painful experience, and despite her ability to finally let go of Harry, Mary was soon in pursuit again

of her earlier unrequited love. Although a good Christian community was important to Mary, it is clear that she gave priority to an
individual relationship with a man. This is what she felt God meant
for her. But the desperation and pain of this search suggests that
Mary was really searching for her self in her relationships. In terms
of Kegan's distinction between Stage 3 fusion and Stage 5 intimacy,
Mary was incapable of intimacy because she had no independent
self to bring to her relationships. As important as relationships
were to Mary, they were the relationships of one whose very self is
constituted by the relationship. Mary *was* her self only in her relationships, only in fusion with another. She was not a strong, independent self capable of transcending and organizing her
relationships. She did not *have* relationships, she *was* her relationships. Her self existed in and thus was subject to her relationships.

If Mary's post-conversion loss of relationships resulted in something less than the suicidal nothingness she had experienced earlier, it was likely because she had the Lord to support her. Though
her relationship to the Lord was just as fused as her relationships
with the other men in her life, the Lord, unlike the others, was
always faithful: "The Lord never forsook me, he was really faithful to
me." Ford-Grabowsky is correct in emphasizing Mary's Christian
faith, and how it changed her life. But Fowler is also correct in
characterizing this faith in terms of Stage 3's uncritical multidimensional symbols. No matter where the Lord led her, and no matter what the results, the Lord was always faithful. With Kegan, we
can understand how this had to be, how Mary's relationship with
the Lord, the fusion of her Interpersonal self with her images of the
Lord, could be nothing other than uncritical. Ford-Grabowsky
assumes that Mary's relationship to the Lord can transcend her
human relational capacities, that grace can overcome developmental limitations. So she sees in Mary's faith only strength. Fowler
assumes that Mary's faith, her relationship to the Lord, is rooted in
her developmental possibilities, and has all the strengths and limitations of her present capacities. If we understand grace as working
within and not above nature, we too may appreciate, through the
perspective of Fowler, Kegan, and the other developmentalists, the
power of Mary's faith in the Lord, but also its necessary developmental limitations and its need for continued expansion. Mary—
not her ego, not her Jungian self, not her Christian self, but Mary

herself—must continue to develop, through the realization of independent identity, toward the fuller dimensions of faith, toward the greater possibilities of genuine *intimacy* in all her relationships, including her relationship with the Lord.

Of course, for Fowler, as we have seen, Mary's possibilities for development are linked to a process of recapitulation. And the above reference to identity and intimacy suggests that we might consider, with Fowler, some of the elements of this process through Erikson's psychosocial developmental lens.

We may begin with Mary's statement, referring to her mother, that "right from the first there was antagonism between us." Given her mother's serious unhappiness during Mary's first years when the foundations of trust are laid, and despite Mary's protestation that "I know she really wanted me," we may suspect that Mary emerged from infancy with more than her share of mistrust. After that bad start, it is not surprising to hear Mary say: "I guess I gave up [on trying to please my mother] at a really early age and just became a really rebellious brat towards my parents."[17] In Erikson's second period, of autonomy vs. shame and doubt, therefore, there may have begun the shameless willfulness and stubborn assertiveness that plagued Mary for the next two decades.

Family relations did not improve much as Mary moved into Erikson's third crisis of initiative vs. guilt: "I remember that I was suicidal from a very early age, and it was always a reaction to my relationship with my mother." This was the emotional baggage Mary brought to elementary school. Her intelligence was recognized, but Fowler got the picture of a lonely girl, burdened with anxiety, shame, and guilt. Mary developed a wonderful friendship with another girl during their preadolescent years, but that ended in abandonment: "I had a really close friend in fifth and sixth grade, and she and I were just inseparable. She became the most popular girl in junior high, and I sort of fell by the wayside. And that really hurt a lot."[18] And nothing improved at home. By the ninth grade Mary found a group of friends and was doing better, but then her family moved from New York to Birmingham, and she never really recovered from the culture shock of the move to the South. She just could not find a satisfying social life.

Despite changing high schools each year, Mary did well enough in her studies, and she went off to begin college after her junior year.

Although at the time it seemed like a good solution to a bad situation, Mary really was not ready for another major change, let alone for college campus life in the sixties: "I was maybe intellectually ready, but not socially or emotionally ready for that change at all. It turned out to be a really devastating experience too." Reflecting on Erikson's crisis of identity, Fowler found little in Mary's high school years that would have contributed to a "clear, integrated and positive image of herself" and much that would have confirmed the "undercurrent of negative self-worth" and anger she brought from childhood.[19]

In college, all of this was heightened as Mary acted out a negative identity in counterdependent rebelliousness, but all the while also searching for truth and love, for something or someone, as Erikson would say, worthy of committing herself to in fidelity. Too often, however, this searching fidelity was exploited and betrayed, and Mary finally hit rock bottom.

After her suicide attempt, Mary experienced what Fowler, while acknowledging its communal limitations, calls a genuine conversion. Mary's "previously scattered and ambiguous vectors of fidelity," he says, "found a focus in Jesus Christ." She was promised that her negative identity and life patterns could be negated, obliterated. So Mary "embarked upon the promise of a new way of life, one in which she could submit her will to the will of the Lord." Unfortunately, from Fowler's faith development perspective, during the next five years in several house churches, "Mary seems not to have grown either in the structuring of her faith or in the strength of her identity...."[20]

To return to the viewpoint of Kegan's self development, we may suggest that as genuine as Mary's conversion experience was, it consisted essentially in an uncritical commitment of fidelity to Jesus Christ, and left Mary's sense of self entirely dependent on this relationship to the Lord as mediated through the various communities she became involved in. In other words, at the object-pole of fidelity Mary made a genuine commitment in her conversion, but at the subject-pole of self and identity, she remained at Stage 3, fused in relationships of dependence, not genuine intimacy, with no independent identity. Now that we have traced elements of Mary's psychosocial development to the point of her conversion, we must review and expand upon the meaning of conversion itself in some detail.

At the end of Chapter 2, I introduced, and in Chapter 7 developed, an understanding of Christian conversion as fourfold: moral, affective, cognitive, and religious. Now, with the goal of clarifying the reality of Mary's conversion, I will relate that four-dimensional understanding to the meanings of conversion presented by Fowler and Ford-Grabowsky.

As we have seen, Fowler is quite explicit in affirming the genuineness of Mary's conversion. He is also explicit about his understanding of conversion. Having distinguished between structure and content in faith, Fowler asserts that "Conversion has to do with changes in the *contents* of faith."[21] Stage change, on the other hand, is structural. Conversion, he writes, is "a significant recentering of one's previous conscious or unconscious images of value and power, and the conscious adoption of a new set of master stories in the commitment to reshape one's life in a new community of interpretation and action."[22] By contents of faith, then, Fowler means centers of value, images of power, and master stories. Conversion, or radical change in these contents, can have several different relationships to structural stages of faith. It can take place in any of the stages, or in the transitions between them. It can lead to structural change or result from it. Theoretically, Fowler suggests six possible relationships between conversion and faith stage change: 1) stage change without conversion, 2) conversion without stage change, 3) conversion that precipitates stage change, 4) stage change that precipitates conversion, 5) conversion that is correlated with stage change, and 6) conversion that blocks stage change.[23]

Within these possibilities, Fowler identifies Mary's key religious experiences as a conversion without stage change. In other words, though Mary underwent no structural change, she did experience a "life-changing shift" in the contents of her faith: "...she gave up her old centers of value, admitted the impoverishment of the images of power on which she had relied and made a self-conscious decision to undertake the reshaping of her life in accordance with a new master story."[24]

We have already discussed Fowler's point that Mary, after her conversion, needed a community's support in a recapitulative process that would transform her developmental strengths. Given this kind of recapitulative process, Fowler suggests that Mary's "conversion would result in a re-grounding of [the strengths of each stage] and their reorientation in light of faith's new center of value, images of power and decisive master-story." This, in Fowler's view, would provide a new, more integrated foundation for a decisive move to the next stage. "...[I]f truly Spirit empowered and thorough," says Fowler, a post-conversion recapitulative experience should free Mary to make "significant movement toward an Individuative-Reflective appropriation of her Christian faith."[25] With such a process, in other words, conversion understood as content change leads, in Fowler's estimation, to structural stage change.

In contrast to Fowler's interpretation, we have seen that Ford-Grabowsky discerns in Mary's experience not one but two conversions. Mary's first conversion, according to Ford-Grabowsky, was from ego to self. Resulting from her spiritual experience while taking LSD, it transformed her into a believer, with religious faith in a monistic God. After several months of a gnostic search for perfect knowledge of the God within, Mary encountered the triune God in 2 Timothy 3:1-7, and in this second conversion her Jungian self was transformed into Hildegard's Christian self. In characterizing Mary's first conversion as a transition from ego to self, Ford-Grabowsky seems to identify this experience with Jung's process of individuation, the process of integrating the whole psyche that usually takes the best part of a person's life. Although the nature of Mary's second conversion as a transition from the Jungian self to the Christian self is even more difficult to specify, it does seem clear that Ford-Grabowsky means to distinguish ego/self/Christian self more in moral-religious qualitative terms than in structural terms.[26] Though ego, self, and Christian self appear to be structural realities, the transitions from ego to self and from self to Christian self are spelled out in terms of content change.

The experience that Ford-Grabowsky specifies as two separate conversions, Fowler brings together as one conversion, though he would probably recognize two "moments" in the total conversion experience. In any case, both Fowler and Ford-Grabowsky, though in very different ways, conceptualize conversion in terms of content change rather than structural change.

In contrast to Fowler's and Ford-Grabowsky's interpretations of conversion as content change, my understanding of conversion focuses rather on structural stage change. I appreciate, of course, the meaning of conversion as content change, and acknowledge the value of Fowler's interpretation. Indeed, I distinguish between horizontal and vertical conversions precisely in order to recognize both content change and structural change as genuine conversions.[27] Horizontal conversions (of content) occur within established horizons; vertical conversions (of structure) create new horizons. If a person's fundamental horizon is defined by a set of existential questions, a change of content or horizontal conversion would be a matter of new answers (content) to old questions within an established horizon. A vertical conversion consists of radically new questions creatively restructuring content (old or new) into a totally new horizon.

While I recognize both types of conversion as genuine and important, I focus on the vertical conversion of structural stage change for several reasons: for example, 1) conversion as content change has received thorough and almost exclusive attention from analysts such as Fowler; 2) conversion as structural change can be involved not only in shifts to new master stories, images, and values, but also—and especially—in transformations *within* the master story a person already has, within, for example, the existing faith of a Christian; and 3) conversion as structural change is necessary in order to realize the radical possibilities and most profound dimensions of religious faith—in this case, of Christian faith.[28]

As we have seen, a person like Mary may experience a conversion to Christian faith in the sense of a commitment to a new master story, images, and values, while remaining at the same structural stage as before the conversion. In such an instance, the person will appropriate the story, images, and values from her or his existing stage or structural orientation, in Mary's case, Stage 3 in terms of both faith and self development. Our earlier examination of conversion in Merton's life indicated, however, that the *fullness* of Christian faith demands radical conversions in the affective, cognitive, moral, and faith dimensions that constitute the highest level of structural development in each of these dimensions, as well as in the whole self. In other words, by its very nature, the *content* of Christian faith requires radical *structural* conversion.

Now, what interpretation of Mary's conversion does the structural understanding of conversion offer? We will look at each dimension of full Christian conversion individually, but we might begin by noting generally that Mary, like Merton, is a fine candidate

for this kind of analysis because her conversion experience followed directly upon a serious personal breakdown, a prerequisite
for major stage change.

First, what can we say about Mary in terms of cognitive conversion? On the evidence of her success in school as well as her articulate interview, it is clear that she is very intelligent. Developmentally,
she obviously has attained a degree of formal operational ability.
When we meet Mary in Fowler's interview, she is capable of making
some fairly sophisticated and astute observations about various persons, events, and situations in her life, but her perspective-taking is
essentially interpersonal, and usually without taking the standpoint
of the other. This limitation also means that Mary had no third-
person perspective for evaluating her relationships with others. In
short, Mary is very intelligent, with formal operations strong
enough to create interpersonal problems for herself, but not powerful enough to deal with them in a satisfactory way.

Without significant development in formal operations, Mary is
incapable of reflecting on herself and, in particular, on her own
cognitive power in the critical way that is essential to cognitive conversion. Only through such critical reflection could Mary discover
the criterion of truth and value in herself, in the normative pattern
of her drive for self-transcendence, *not* in some external authority.[29]
Thus Mary's faith and conversion, as genuine as they are, remain
uncritical, and they are likely to remain so without something of
the kind of recapitulative care Fowler recommends. We shall now
see that all this it true, too, of Mary's moral conversion.

While it is clear that Mary has not experienced cognitive conversion, it is just as clear that she has experienced basic moral conversion—that her conversion, though uncritical, is to basic Christian
values. Despite her continuing difficulties, Mary has opted for Christian value as her criterion for decisions: "I put down my pride and
made a decision that I was going to believe in Jesus Christ and follow
him."[30] Mary's effort to find and follow God's will is a persistent
theme throughout her interview.[31] We have already seen in Chapter 1
how Ford-Grabowsky detects in Mary's post-conversion life the two
factors Hildegard associates with the Christian self: Christian faith
and Christian character.[32] Ford-Grabowsky reminds us that not even
the most bitter suffering could shake Mary's strong faith. And Ford-
Grabowsky highlights many of the Christian virtues Mary imitated:

love, forgiveness, fortitude, and—in keeping with the uncritical nature of her conversion—obedience. Mary has *structurally* committed herself to value, and, in *content,* specifically to the values and images of the Christian story in the person of Jesus Christ.

Lacking cognitive conversion, Mary's moral conversion, though a genuine commitment to value, is not what I named in Chapter 7 a critical moral conversion. In terms of Kohlberg's developmental schema, it has all the earmarks of Level II conventional morality—a conversion to conventional Christian values. And it seems to be precisely the uncritical nature of her Stage 3, interpersonal moral conversion that accounts for most of Mary's post-conversion difficulties—her dependence on external authority because she has not found authority in her own self-transcending judgments, because she has not discovered herself as the author of her life's moral script.

Since the affective dimension of Mary's life is, at best, at least as complicated as most people's, our analysis of it and of the possibility of affective conversion must be complex. My reflections will be from the developmental perspectives of Erikson and Kegan.

Although all of Erikson's psychosocial tasks involve the affective dimension in various important ways, I have identified the young adult task or crisis of intimacy as central to affective conversion. Here the young adult who has established a sense of identity now risks that identity by offering to share his or her self in mutuality with another. As we have seen, Mary wants to share her self, but has no consolidated, independent sense of identity to bring to a truly mutual relationship. Rather, she is trying to find herself in relationships and, as we noted from Kegan's perspective, has experienced, even after her conversion, the difficulties associated with dependent relationships of fusion. In sum, affectively, Mary has great desire for intimacy, but her possibility of realizing that desire is limited by the nature of her self and the quality of her pattern of relating. This is just as true of Mary's relationship with God as it is of her relationship with other persons. Short of therapy, only something like Fowler's recapitulation process is likely to help Mary gain the strength of independent identity necessary for the challenge of true intimacy—and affective conversion. Then her desire to give of her self will be liberated from the bonds of self-interest needs, and the fundamental thrust of her Christian moral conversion will be realized with significant consistency.

As I specified with Lonergan in the previous chapter, religious conversion is "other-worldly falling in love." For Christians who understand God as love itself, religious conversion in this sense is falling in love with love. These words may have the aroma of foolish romanticism, but radical Christian belief overturns the conventional wisdom of the old popular song. Rather than "falling for make-believe," Christian understanding of God affirms that falling in love with love is falling for truth itself. Falling in love with God *is* falling in love with both love and truth. Religious conversion is giving one's life over without reservation to the desire to love and the search for truth, to the hunger for goodness and the thirst for justice.

We have seen how religious conversion in this sense is adumbrated in the developmental perspective by the highest stages of Kohlberg (7) and Fowler (6), and how this fullness of development is optimally a response to Erikson's crisis of integrity in one's mature years. Although it seems clear that Mary loves God and wants to do God's will by following Jesus, it is equally clear that Mary's development is consistently at Stage 3 across the board, far short of the developmental conditions for the possibility of religious conversion in the full, radical sense.

We can also approach this point from the angle of autonomy and surrender. From this perspective, religious conversion can be understood as the total surrender of the claim to absolute autonomy. Personal autonomy is affirmed, but relativized. To cite another homely scholastic dictum, "You can't give what you don't have" (*Nemo dat quod non habet*). Just as affective conversion requires independent identity in order to give one's self to others, religious conversion requires personal autonomy in order to surrender one's self fully to God in love. As God's grace continues to be communicated through personal relationships, one day Mary may attain the personal autonomy necessary to surrender her self completely to God. Until then, Mary, like most of us, tries her best to let God lead her to such autonomy and surrender.

Appendix:

Self-Transcendence in Counseling

This appendix will relate self-transcendence to two widely known and successful presentations in counselor education: the three-stage model proposed by Gerard Egan[1] and the various therapeutic approaches summarized by Gerald Corey.[2]

From what has been said about self-transcendence in this study, my option for a humanistic, existential, person-centered orientation to counseling is probably clear. While all of the characteristics Corey specifies for this orientation may not fit, their central thrust is expressed in the concept of the desire for self-transcendence. Briefly summarized from Corey, this central thrust includes (1) the capacity for self-awareness, (2) freedom and responsibility, (3) commitment, (4) choice, (5) discovering one's identity and meaningfully relating to others, (6) the search for meaning, values, purpose, and goals, (7) respect of the person, (8) actualization of the inborn urge to become an authentic person, (9) painful struggle of the continuous growth toward the maturity of inner-directedness and relational autonomy, and (10) self-creation.

From the perspective of the earlier delineation of the desire for self-transcendence in terms of questions and responding activities, four levels of the self-transcending person may be specified: (1) experiential, (2) intelligent, (3) rational, and (4) responsible or existential (see Figure 2, left column, reading from bottom up; this chart correlates levels of Lonergan's view of self-transcendence with associated stages in Egan's counseling model, which are then correlated with task-appropriate therapeutic approaches). Whereas the focus of the first three levels is cognitive, the fourth or highest level focuses on all those other dimensions of the person called existential: value, freedom, responsibility, decision, choice, commitment, fidelity, love, self-creation.

For all the reasons given by Carl Rogers and other humanistic therapists, as well as for personal philosophical and theological convictions, the view presented here shares the person-centered approach's fundamental respect for the person as a basic value in counseling. That is the foundation of everything done with a client. Given this humanistic, existential, person-centered orientation of counseling for self-transcendence, let us now shift to Egan's three-stage model and discuss its various phases in terms of the four levels of the self-transcending person and in terms of several different approaches to counseling and therapy. What will be outlined here, then, is an eclectic approach to counseling, but not a spineless eclecticism that desperately grabs a little of this and a little of that because it has no clear direction. Rather, it is an eclecticism that has the desire for self-transcendence as its backbone and the best aspects of many approaches for its flesh and blood. This is a counseling approach that knows where it is going. However, realizing that the multidimensional person exists on many different levels, it recognizes that it too must be multidimensional. Therefore, it is a multistage process that utilizes helpful aspects of many therapeutic perspectives, depending on their ability to promote development and self-transcendence. Notice that in this approach the client's self-transcendence is not only the goal of counseling and criterion of authentic development, but that self-transcendence also defines the very direction and stages of the counseling process itself.

The first phase activities of Egan's Stage 1—Attending and Listening—are clearly Rogerian preconditions for any effective therapeutic relationship. They also relate directly to the first level of the desire for self-transcendence. Here the basic precept is: Be attentive to your experience. Obviously, self-transcendence is as important to the counselor as it is to the client. Therefore, here the counselor is listening and trying to attend to the client's experience (verbal and nonverbal) as closely as possible in order to help the client do the same for himself or herself. For some clients, and some problems,

SELF-TRANSCENDENCE Lonergan	THREE-STAGE MODEL Egan	THERAPEUTIC APPROACHES Corey
EXISTENTIAL-RESPONSIBLE Deciding to Act Value, Love	Evaluation Implementation b) Second Prase	REALITY BEHAVIOR
RATIONAL Judging Truth	Sequencing ⌐ Choosing ├—Programs Identifying ⌐ a) First Phase 3. ACTION	BEHAVIOR
INTELLIGENT Understanding Meaning	Realistic Goals General Statement of Aim Declaration of Intent b) Second Phase	

	Immediacy
	Self-Sharing
	Advanced Empathy
	Information Giving
	Summarizing
	a) First Phase
	2. DEVELOPING NEW
	   PERSPECTIVES AND
	   SETTING GOALS
		GESTALT
		TRANSACTIONAL
		  ANALYSIS
		
		COGNITIVE
		RATIONAL-EMOTIVE

	Accurate Empathy b) Second Phase	PSYCHOANALYTIC
EXPERIENTIAL Attending Data	Attending and Listening a) First Phase 1. PROBLEM EXPLORATION AND CLARIFICATION	CLIENT-CENTERED

FIGURE 2

Relationships Among Self-Transcendence, Three-Stage Model,
and Therapeutic Approaches

psychoanalytic techniques such as free association may be useful (even necessary) to help the client attend to certain kinds of experience.

Of course, as counselors, we do not just listen and attend to the client's experience. We follow the desire for self-transcendence to the second level of intelligence, trying to understand that experience and trying to help the client understand it (primary empathy and clarification). Now, in Egan's model, all this is done as building blocks for later stages of the counseling process, but even this Stage 1 activity has its own therapeutic value for the client.

The desire for self-transcending understanding is extended as we move into Egan's Stage 2. Here the aim is for the client to develop a new, more objective perspective with a dynamic understanding aimed at goal-oriented action. This new perspective and understanding is the purpose of all the counselor's challenging activities at this stage: summarizing, information-giving, advanced empathy, self-sharing, immediacy. Specific techniques of many different approaches may be appropriate to facilitate understanding at this stage. Rational-Emotive Therapy is perhaps the most obvious of the approaches useful for transforming a client's perspective and bringing about dynamic understanding. It is difficult to imagine a technique more explicitly aimed at effecting a new perspective and understanding than that of disputing irrational beliefs. Likewise, the Cognitive Therapy of Beck and others zeroes in on distorted and unrealistic thinking and tries to restructure thought patterns through alternative interpretations in order to reshape one's emotions and reorganize one's behavior. Transactional Analysis is another obvious candidate for implementation at this stage of goal-directed self-understanding. Rescripting life scripts is perhaps the clearest example we have of the interest of Transactional Analysis in transforming cognitive-emotional perspectives through insight. Although the Gestalt approach tends to deemphasize cognitive factors (at least those of the explicit, conceptual sort favored by RET), its interest in the expansion of awareness is an acknowledgment that a certain kind of nonconceptual understanding is necessary for personality change. For example, the top dog/underdog split with an empty chair is one of many techniques Gestalt employs toward the goal of expanding awareness and understanding of conflict and polarities.

All the ways Stage 2 challenges toward dynamic self-understanding in its first phase are for the sake of setting clear, concrete goals in its second phase. This second phase—moving from understanding, through declaration of intent and general statement of aim, to realistic goals—may be correlated with the third level of the self-transcending person, the rational level of judging. For the final purpose of Stage 2 is the translation of new understanding into a goal that client and counselor judge realistic.[3]

In Egan's Stage 3, Action, there are five key tasks related to programming goals for action. The first phase of this stage—identifying, choosing, and sequencing programs (practical ways of achieving goals)—continues to emphasize the cognitive levels of understanding and judging. Divergent thinking, brainstorming, and other means of identifying program possibilities are all exercises of creative understanding, of going beyond the given through the power of imagination and insight. Selecting one program from among the many possibilities requires a process of evaluation (with explicit criteria) leading to the judgment that this is the best (that is, most realistic, and so on) program for this person in this situation. Finally, the fine-tuning of a program (distinguishing subprograms/goals and relating them all to each other and to the main goal and program) is also a cognitive matter of understanding and judgment. Behavior Therapy has led the way in developing sophisticated methods for programming goals. It has also been a leader in the area of effective program implementation, a key task in the second phase of Stage 3.

Implementation and evaluation of programs are the final steps in Egan's model. Although behavioral techniques (reinforcement, assertiveness training, contracts, and so forth) can be very helpful at the implementation stage, attention here will be on the contribution of Reality Therapy, because the focus shifts at this stage from the self-transcending person's levels of knowing to the level of deciding to act. Here the client must assume the responsibility of putting his or her new perspective, goal, and program into action. The client can and should be supported through this risky business in many ways, but finally it is the client's personal decision to move into concrete action that counts; no technique or no other person can do this for her or him. No other approach is quite as strong as Reality Therapy on this fundamental issue of personal responsibility. Glasser focuses explicitly on the central issues of what Lonergan names the fourth level of the self-transcending person, the level of decision and action, the existential level of freedom and responsibility. Glasser emphasizes not only personal responsibility, but also values, decision, commitment, action, identity, and autonomy. And he accepts no excuses. Finally, evaluation means a return to the cognitive levels in order to review critically the program and its implementation in terms of goal fulfillment. Reassessment can lead to reprogramming and reimplementation.

This, then, in bare bones, is counseling for self-transcendence. It is an approach guided by the developmental goal of relational autonomy. It is eclectic in the critical sense of employing any and every means that can contribute to the achievement of that goal. The stages of Egan's overall model reflect the four basic levels of the developing person striving for self-transcendence: (1) attending to experience, (2) dynamic understanding of self and world, (3) judging goals and programs, and (4) deciding to implement a program in action. Counseling that follows this paradigm not only guides a client to develop toward the greater self-transcendence of relational autonomy, but also provides in the counseling process itself a concrete model of that very self-transcendence. Egan's emphasis on problem-solving may suggest a rather narrow focus on pedestrian issues of daily life, but interpreting his model in terms of development and self-transcendence suggests that it is applicable to problems as big as life itself: the personal problem of living with others more attentively, more creatively, more realistically, more responsibly, more lovingly—all, for the religious person, in response to the gracious power of an immanent God, who is self-transcendence itself.

NOTES

INTRODUCTION

1. On the God within, interiority, and ascent, see Denys Turner, *The Darkness of God* (Cambridge: Cambridge University Press, 1995), pp. 50-101. Also see Anne Hunsaker Hawkins, *Archetypes of Conversion: The Autobiographies of Augustine, Bunyan, and Merton* (Lewisburg, Pa.: Bucknell University Press, 1985). For Merton's admiration of Augustine and his *Confessions,* see Thomas Merton, *Run to the Mountain,* The Journals of Thomas Merton 1, ed. Patrick Hart (San Francisco: HarperSanFrancisco, 1996 [1995]), pp. 3, 21, 42, 83.

2. See James W. Fowler, *Faithful Change: The Personal and Public Challenges of Postmodern Life* (Nashville: Abingdon, 1996), p. 206.

3. Philip Sheldrake, *Befriending Our Desires* (Notre Dame, Ind.: Ave Maria, 1994), p. 7.

4. For the above points on desire, see Sheldrake, pp. 10, 21, 100, 101.

5. I differ somewhat in language here from Sheldrake, who associates "ought" with *aspirations* for external ideals (duties, unrealistic dreams) in contrast to *desires* which are "more intrinsic to the reality of each person" (p. 13), but I think we agree on the substantive point.

6. See Sheldrake, p. 126.

7. For an important American critique, see Mark Taylor, *Erring: A Postmodern A/theology* (Chicago: University of Chicago Press, 1984), who rejects a solitary self that defines itself in opposition to other isolated selves and argues for a view in which "subjects are never isolated monads but are always reciprocally related" (p. 135). For a helpful discussion of

contemporary critiques of the self, see David Tracy, *Plurality and Ambiguity* (San Francisco: Harper & Row, 1987), pp. 82, 89-90. Also see Dermot A. Lane's reflections on "The Self in Crisis" in his *Keeping Hope Alive* (New York: Paulist, 1996), pp. 25-41; and Anthony C. Thiselton, *Interpreting God and the Postmodern Self* (Grand Rapids: Eerdmans, 1995), pp. 11-17. For a developmental perspective on this contemporary criticism, see Robert Kegan, *In Over Our Heads: The Mental Demands of Modern Life* (Cambridge: Harvard University Press, 1994), pp. 324-34.

The self I will be considering here is not an isolated, theoretical thinking subject but is always understood, with John Macmurray, to be a practical self as agent that exists only in dynamic relation with others. See the two volumes of Macmurray's Gifford Lectures, The Form of the Personal: *The Self as Agent* (London: Faber and Faber, 1957), pp. 11-12, 21-23, 31, and *Persons in Relation* (London: Faber and Faber, 1961), pp. 12, 17. Also see Paul Ricoeur, *Oneself as Another*, trans. Kathleen Blamey (Chicago: University of Chicago Press, 1992), for another penetrating analysis of otherness as "constitutive of selfhood as such" (p. 3).

The present study seeks to locate the foundations of pastoral counseling and spiritual direction not in alien statements or propositions, but in the self, in its radical desire for relational self-transcendence, and in its dynamic personal operations—all empirical realities that can be attended to, understood, and verified by the counselor or director in her or his own experience.

8. M. Scott Peck, "Foreword" in Robert J. Wicks, Richard D. Parsons, and Donald E. Capps, eds., *Clinical Handbook of Pastoral Counseling* (New York: Paulist, 1985), p. 1. For a recent integration of psychological and theological perspectives, see Leroy T. Howe, *The Image of God: A Theology of Pastoral Care and Counseling* (Nashville: Abingdon, 1995). For another effort at integration in a somewhat different context, see Daniel A. Helminiak, *The Human Core of Spirituality: Mind as Psyche and Spirit* (Albany: State University of New York, 1996).

9. Donald S. Browning, "Introduction to Pastoral Counseling" in Wicks et al., *Clinical Handbook*, p. 6.

10. Clyde V. Steckel, "Directions in Pastoral Counseling" in Wicks et al., *Clinical Handbook*, p. 32.

11. See Charles Taylor, *Sources of the Self: The Making of the Modern Identity* (Cambridge: Harvard University Press, 1989), pp. x, 32-40.

12. In addition to many articles, some cited below, my work on develop-

ment and conversion is in my *Conscience: Development and Self-Transcendence* (Birmingham, Ala.: Religious Education Press, 1981) and *Christian Conversion: A Developmental Interpretation of Autonomy and Surrender* (New York: Paulist, 1986).

CHAPTER 1

1. James W. Fowler, *Stages of Faith: The Psychology of Human Development and the Quest for Meaning* (San Francisco: Harper & Row, 1981), pp. 217-68.

2. Ibid., p. 263.

3. Mary Ford-Grabowsky, "Flaws in Faith Development Theory," *Religious Education* 82 (Winter 1987): 80-93. Also see, by the same author, "What Developmental Phenomenon is Fowler Studying?" *Journal of Psychology and Christianity* 5/3 (Fall 1986): 5-13; "The Fullness of the Christian Faith Experience: Dimensions Missing in Faith Development Theory," *Journal of Pastoral Care* 41/1 (March 1987): 39-47; and "The Journey of a Pilgrim: An Alternative to Fowler," *Living Light* 24 (March 1988): 242-54.

4. Ford-Grabowsky, "Flaws," p. 84.

5. Ibid., p. 86.

6. Ibid., p. 89.

7. Ibid., p. 91.

8. Ibid. Actually, Fowler does not say that one *ought* to be at any particular stage at a given age, but rather gives a typical minimal age for each stage.

9. Ibid., p. 84.

CHAPTER 2

1. See E. Brooks Holifield, *A History of Pastoral Care in America: From Salvation to Self-Realization* (Nashville: Abingdon, 1983), p. 12.

2. See ibid., p. 57.

3. See ibid., pp. 69, 76.

4. See ibid., pp. 84-85, 94.

5. See ibid., p. 99.

6. See ibid., pp. 129-30, 132, 141, 143, 151.

7. See ibid., pp. 156-57.

8. See ibid., pp. 159, 178.

9. See ibid., pp. 160, 189-90, 208.

10. See ibid., pp. 222, 223.

11. Rollo May, *The Art of Counseling* (Nashville: Cokesbury, 1939).

12. See Holifield, p. 252.

13. See ibid., p. 257.

14. See ibid., p. 288.

15. See ibid., pp. 291-92.

16. See ibid., p. 294.

17. Carl R. Rogers, *Counseling and Psychotherapy* (Boston: Houghton Mifflin, 1942).

18. See Holifield, p. 295.

19. See ibid., pp. 296-97.

20. Carl R. Rogers, *Client-Centered Therapy* (Boston: Houghton Mifflin, 1951).

21. See Holifield, pp. 297-98.

22. Seward Hiltner, *Pastoral Counseling* (New York and Nashville: Abingdon-Cokesbury, 1949), p. 19.

23. See ibid., pp. 26-32.

24. See ibid., pp. 47-54.

25. See ibid., pp. 71-77.

26. Carroll A. Wise, *Pastoral Counseling: Its Theory and Practice* (New York: Harper, 1951), p. 45.

27. See ibid., pp. 51, 22, 53-54, 5-6.

28. See ibid., pp. 116, 118, 165-66.

29. Paul E. Johnson, *Psychology of Pastoral Care* (New York and Nashville: Abingdon-Cokesbury, 1953), pp. 34-36.

30. See ibid., pp. 27-30.

31. Ibid., p. 24.

32. See ibid., pp. 100, 101, 17.

33. Wayne E. Oates, *The Christian Pastor* (Philadelphia: Westminster, 1951), pp. 26, 32.

34. See ibid., pp. 116-38, 130.

35. See Seward Hiltner, *Preface to Pastoral Theology* (Nashville: Abingdon, 1958) and Seward Hiltner and Lowell G. Colston, *The Context of Pastoral Counseling* (Nashville: Abingdon, 1961); also see Holifield, pp. 312-13.

36. Howard J. Clinebell, Jr., *Basic Types of Pastoral Counseling* (Nashville: Abingdon, 1966), p. 23.

37. See ibid., pp. 28-36.

38. See ibid., pp. 18, 18-19, 20.

39. Ibid., p. 46.

40. Howard J. Clinebell, Jr., *Basic Types of Pastoral Care and Counseling* (rev. ed.; Nashville: Abingdon, 1984), p. 26.

41. See ibid., pp. 32-33.

42. See ibid., pp. 106, 110.

CHAPTER 3

1. M. Müller and A. Halder, "Person" in *Sacramentum Mundi*, ed. K. Rahner *et al.* (New York: Herder, 1969), 6:404.

2. Descartes' attention to interiority must be clearly distinguished from Augustine's or, in this study, from Lonergan's and Merton's. Merton, for example, characterizes Descartes' subject as a "solipsistic bubble of awareness" (Thomas Merton, *Zen and the Birds of Appetite* [New York: New Directions, 1968], p. 22). Paradigmatic for modern philosophy, this self is really an object of interior perception, not the conscious self-as-subject we will see later in this chapter. For a rigorous analysis of the self in modern philosophy, see Ricoeur, *Oneself as Another.*

3. For the continuing significance of Locke, as well as for a helpful brief history of "person" in Western philosophy, see Warren Bourgeois, *Persons: What Philosophers Say About You* (Waterloo, Ontario: Wilfrid Laurier University Press, 1995), esp. pp. 81-87.

4. Erik H. Erikson, *Identity: Youth and Crisis* (New York: Norton, 1968), p. 218. For a detailed analysis of the relation of ego, self, and conscious "I," see Walter E. Conn, "Erikson's 'Identity': An Essay on the Psychological Foundations of Religious Ethics," *Zygon* 14/2 (June 1979): 125-34.

The meanings of "conscious" and "unconscious" are very tricky. Although this distinction is commonplace in psychology and ordinary language, it would usually be more accurate to distinguish within consciousness between that which is explicitly objectified and that which is tacit and unobjectified. Unlike the strictly unconscious growth of toenails, much that we characterize as "unconscious" is conscious but unobjectified, and can in various ways be rendered explicitly conscious. On the "twilight of what is conscious but not objectified," see Bernard Lonergan, *Method in Theology* (New York: Herder and Herder, 1972), p. 34.

5. Erikson, *Identity: Youth and Crisis*, p. 218.

6. Herbert Fingarette, *The Transformation of the Self* (New York: Harper & Row, 1965), pp. 26, 27-28.

7. See ibid., pp. 78-79, 83-84, 89.

8. Erikson, *Identity: Youth and Crisis*, p. 218.

9. Erik H. Erikson, "The Galilean Sayings and the Sense of 'I'," *Yale Review* 70 (Spring 1981): 321-62, at 323, quoting from William James, *Psychology: The Briefer Course*, ed. G. Allport (Notre Dame, Ind.: University of Notre Dame Press, 1985 [1892]), p. 43.

10. James, *Psychology: The Briefer Course*, p. 70.

11. See Owen Flanagan, *Consciousness Reconsidered* (Cambridge: MIT Press, 1992), p. 194.

12. See Bernard Lonergan, "Christ as Subject: A Reply" in *Collection*, ed. F. E. Crowe (New York: Herder and Herder, 1967), pp. 164-97. For an illuminating consideration of the importance of "consciousness as experience" in the contemporary continental philosophical context, see Fred Lawrence, "The Fragility of Consciousness: Lonergan and the Postmodern Concern for the Other," *Theological Studies* 54/1 (March 1993): 55-94, esp. 68-71. For helpful American philosophical discussion and review of scientific perspectives, see John R. Searle, *The Rediscovery of the Mind* (Cambridge: MIT Press, 1992) and *The Mystery of Consciousness* (New York: New York Review of Books, 1997).

13. For a contrasting view of subjective self-presence, see Taylor, *Erring*: "the subject thinks about itself thinking about an object that seems to be different from itself" (p. 39). For a consideration of further details and complexities of Lonergan's theory of consciousness, see the essays in the symposium "Topology and Economy of Consciousness," *Method: Journal of Lonergan Studies* 13/2 (Fall 1995).

14. A patient in a "persistent vegetative state" is not a "self" because totally without consciousness. Further, though legally alive (not totally brain dead) and deserving of respect, it may be wondered whether such a patient is any longer strictly speaking a "person" because *permanently* without the potential for consciousness as a result of severe, irreversible cerebral damage (in contrast to a patient who because *temporarily* anesthetized for major surgery is not a conscious self but is still a person with the potential for consciousness).

15. James, *Psychology: The Briefer Course*, p. 334.

16. See Bernard Lonergan, *Insight: A Study in Human Understanding* (2d ed.; New York: Philosophical Library, 1958), pp. 319-28. For a helpful analysis of self-affirmation, see Joseph Flanagan, *Quest for Self-Knowledge: An Essay in Lonergan's Philosophy* (Toronto: University of Toronto Press, 1997), pp. 131-36.

17. James, *Psychology: The Briefer Course,* p. 334.

18. Ibid., p. 43.

19. Ibid., p. 44. On the dipolar self and gender identity, see Sidney Callahan, "Does Gender Make a Difference in Moral Decision Making?" *Second*

Opinion 17/2 (October 1991): 67-77, esp. 70-71: "Gender identity is only one aspect of self, an aspect of the bodily and social me, of the self as known....While the I and me are a unified self, the self as knower, the self of selves appears to be without gender" (70).

20. James, *Psychology: The Briefer Course*, p. 45.

21. Ibid., pp. 46, 47.

22. Ibid., p. 48.

23. Ibid., p. 50.

24. Ibid., p. 57 (entire quotation italicized in original).

25. See ibid., pp. 58, 59.

26. The word "thing" is used here in the ordinary informal sense. For a technical meaning of "thing" as an intelligible, concrete unity distinguished from "body," see Lonergan, *Insight*, pp. 245-59.

CHAPTER 4

1. See Sigmund Freud, *The Ego and the Id* (1923), Standard Edition, 19 (London: Hogarth, 1961).

2. See Heinz Hartmann, *Ego Psychology and the Problem of Adaptation* (New York: International Universities Press, 1958 [1939]), pp. 3-21, 74-79, 100-08.

3. See C. G. Jung, *Two Essays on Analytical Psychology* (1916), Complete Works, 7 (Princeton, N.J.: Princeton University Press, 1977): 173-87, and "On the Nature of the Psyche" (1946), Complete Works, 8 (Princeton, N.J.: Princeton University Press, 1969): 159-234, esp. 224-26.

4. See Melanie Klein, *The Psycho-Analysis of Children* (London: Hogarth, 1973 [1932]), pp. 245-67.

5. See Harry Stack Sullivan, *The Interpersonal Theory of Psychiatry* (New York: Norton, 1953), pp. 158-71.

6. See Karen Horney, *Neurosis and Human Growth: The Struggle Toward Self-Realization* (New York: Norton, 1950), pp. 155-75.

7. Ronald Fairbairn, *An Object-Relations Theory of Personality* (New York:

Basic Books, 1954), p. 137. For an especially illuminating study of object-relations theory and religious faith, see John McDargh, *Psychoanalytic Object Relations Theory and the Study of Religion: On Faith and the Imaging of God* (Lanham, Md.: University Press of America, 1983). Also see John McDargh, "The Life of the Self in Christian Spirituality and Contemporary Psychoanalysis," *Horizons* 11/2 (Fall 1984): 344-60.

8. See D. W. Winnicott, *The Maturational Process and the Facilitating Environment* (New York: International Universities Press, 1965), esp. 140-52.

9. See Heinz Hartmann, *Essays in Ego Psychology* (New York: International Universities Press, 1964), p. 127.

10. See Edith Jacobson, *The Self and the Object World* (New York: International Universities Press, 1964).

11. See Otto Kernberg, *Object-Relations Theory and Clinical Psychoanalysis* (New York: Jason Aronson, 1976), pp. 19-54.

12. See Margaret Mahler, Fred Pine, and Anni Bergman, *The Psychological Birth of the Human Infant: Symbiosis and Individuation* (New York: Basic Books, 1975), pp. 39-120.

13. See Daniel Stern, *The Interpersonal World of the Infant* (New York: Basic Books, 1985), pp. 37-182. Also see Fowler, *Faithful Change,* pp. 26-43.

14. See Heinz Kohut, *The Restoration of the Self* (New York: International Universities Press, 1977).

15. See G. S. Klein, *Psychoanalytic Theory* (New York: International Universities Press, 1976).

16. James Masterson, *The Search for the Real Self* (New York: Free Press, 1988), p. 23 (entire quotation italicized in original).

17. Ibid., p. 24.

18. See ibid., pp. 42-46.

19. See Harry Guntrip, *Schizoid Phenomena, Object-Relations and the Self* (New York: International Universities Press, 1968).

20. Erik H. Erikson, "Identity, Psychosocial," *International Encyclopedia of the Social Sciences* 7:61-65, at 61.

On the development of identity and self, also see Ernest S. Wolf, "Self, Idealization, and the Development of Values," pp. 56-77, and Augusto Blasi, "The Development of Identity: Some Implications for Moral Functioning," pp. 99-122, in Gil Noam and Thomas Wren, eds., *The Moral Self: Building a Better Paradigm* (Cambridge: MIT Press, 1993).

21. William James, *The Letters of William James*, ed. Henry James (Boston: Atlantic Monthly Press, 1920), 1: 199.

22. Erikson, "Identity, Psychosocial," p. 61.

23. Erik H. Erikson, *Identity and the Life Cycle*, Psychological Issues, 1 (New York: International Universities Press, 1959), p. 102.

24. Erik H. Erikson, "Life Cycle," *International Encyclopedia of the Social Sciences* 9:286-92, at 290.

25. Erik H. Erikson, *Childhood and Society* (2d ed.; New York: Norton, 1963), pp. 261-62.

26. Quoted in Harry Guntrip, *Psychoanalytic Theory, Therapy, and the Self* (New York: Basic Books, 1973), p. 92.

27. See ibid., p. 86.

28. Erikson, *Childhood and Society*, p. 192.

29. See Guntrip, *Psychoanalytic Theory, Therapy, and the Self*, pp. 50, 42.

30. Michael Polanyi, *The Study of Man* (Chicago: University of Chicago Press, 1963), pp. 46, 92, 62.

31. Lonergan, *Insight*, pp. 472, 473.

32. Ibid., pp. 474, 475.

33. Ibid., p. 477.

34. James, *Psychology: The Briefer Course*, p. 44.

35. For a consideration of this theme from the perspective of Ignatian spirituality, see John English, *Choosing Life: The Significance of Personal History in Decision-Making* (New York: Paulist, 1978). For an interesting discussion of the dipolar self in Augustine's *Confessions* (the present exploring subject and literary creator; the past explored object and literary creation), see René E. Fortin, *Gaining Upon Certainty: Selected Literary*

Criticism, ed. Brian Barbour and Rodney Delasanta (Providence, R.I.: Providence College Press, 1995), pp. 292-96.

CHAPTER 5

1. See Henri J. M. Nouwen, *Reaching Out: The Three Movements of the Spiritual Life* (Garden City, N.Y.: Doubleday, 1975).

2. Victor Frankl, *Man's Search for Meaning: An Introduction to Logotherapy*, trans. I. Lasch (2d ed.; New York: Washington Square Press, 1963 [1959]), p. 175.

3. See Conn, *Christian Conversion*, pp. 19-25.

4. Kegan, *In Over Our Heads*, p. 9.

5. See Conn, *Conscience: Development and Self-Transcendence*, pp. 202-8.

6. Lonergan, *Method in Theology*, pp. 240, 242.

7. Thomas Merton, *Seeds of Contemplation* (New York: Dell, 1960 [1949]), pp. 20, 22, 41, 40, 23.

8. Thomas Merton, *New Seeds of Contemplation* (New York: New Directions, 1972 [1961]), pp. 7, 38.

9. See Anne E. Carr, *A Search for Wisdom and Spirit: Thomas Merton's Theology of the Self* (Notre Dame, Ind.: University of Notre Dame Press, 1988), p. 125.

10. Thomas Merton, "The Inner Experience" (unpublished manuscript at Thomas Merton Studies Center, Bellarmine College, Louisville, KY), pp. 6-7. Edited selections from this manuscript appear in *Cistercian Studies* 18 (1983) and 19 (1984).

11. Carr, *Search for Wisdom and Spirit*, p. 143.

12. See Taylor, *Sources of the Self*, pp. x, 32-40.

13. Such scriptural passages have linguistic and textual problems that are beyond our present scope. See, e.g., John L. McKenzie's comments on "self" in Mt 16 in *The Jerome Biblical Commentary*, ed. Raymond E. Brown, Joseph A. Fitzmyer, and Roland E. Murphy (Englewood Cliffs, N.J.: Prentice-Hall, 1968).

14. See Erich Fromm, *The Art of Loving* (2d ed.; New York: Bantam, 1963 [1956]), pp. 48-49.

15. Ibid., pp. 50, 51.

16. See ibid. For a very helpful consideration of self, sin, and narcissism, see Donald Capps, *The Depleted Self: Sin in a Narcissistic Age* (Minneapolis: Fortress, 1993).

17. Fromm, p. 50.

CHAPTER 6

1. Jean Piaget, *The Origins of Intelligence in Children*, trans. M. Cook (New York: Norton, 1963 [1952; French 1936]), p. 6.

2. See John Flavell, *The Developmental Psychology of Jean Piaget* (New York: Van Nostrand Reinhold, 1963), p. 59.

3. Jean Piaget, *The Construction of Reality in the Child,* trans. M. Cook (New York: Ballantine, 1971 [1954; French 1937]), p. 396.

4. Flavell, p. 60.

5. Piaget, *Construction*, pp. x-xi.

6. Jean Piaget, *Six Psychological Studies,* trans. A. Tenzor and ed. D. Elkind (New York: Random House Vintage, 1968 [French 1964]), pp. 12-13.

7. See Flavell, p. 61.

8. See Piaget, *Construction*, pp. 401-2, xi, and *Six Studies*, pp. 13-14.

9. Piaget, *Six Studies*, pp. 16-17.

10. Erikson, *Identity: Youth and Crisis*, p. 93.

11. Erikson, *Childhood and Society*, p. 249.

12. Erikson, *Identity: Youth and Crisis*, pp. 118, 115; also see p. 116 and *Childhood and Society*, p. 250.

13. Erikson, *Childhood and Society*, p. 249.

14. Erikson, *Identity: Youth and Crisis*, p. 99.

15. Robert Kegan, *The Evolving Self: Problems and Process in Human Development* (Cambridge: Harvard University Press, 1982), p. 77. In his most recent work, *In Over Our Heads*, Kegan shifts linguistically from "selves" to "orders of consciousness," but the substance of his thought remains, though more nuanced. For example, within each order he now distinguishes and integrates cognitive, interpersonal, and intrapersonal lines of development. For a recent consideration of Kegan's theory within a broad developmental context, see Gerald Young, *Adult Development, Therapy, and Culture: A Postmodern Synthesis* (New York: Plenum, 1997), pp. 46-59. For another important contribution to a unified developmental perspective, see Hans G. Furth, *Knowledge as Desire: An Essay on Freud and Piaget* (New York: Columbia University Press, 1987).

16. Kegan, *Evolving Self* pp. 81-82.

17. Fowler, *Faithful Change*, pp. 132, 92, 111.

18. Erikson, *Identity: Youth and Crisis*, p. 119. For valuable reflections on the superego, see Hans W. Loewald, *Papers on Psychoanalysis* (New Haven: Yale University Press, 1980), esp. p. 273, where conscience, though understood as the "mouthpiece" of the superego, speaks to us "from the point of view of the inner future which we envision."

19. Erikson, "Life Cycle," p. 289.

20. Erikson, *Identity and the Life Cycle,* p. 124.

21. Erik H. Erikson, *Insight and Responsibility* (New York: Norton, 1964), p. 124 (entire quotation italicized in original).

22. Lawrence Kohlberg, "Moral Stages and Moralization: The Cognitive-Developmental Approach" in Thomas Lickona, ed., *Moral Development and Behavior: Theory, Research, and Social Issues* (New York: Holt, Rinehart and Winston, 1976), pp. 31-53, at 33.

23. James W. Fowler, "Stages in Faith: The Structural-Developmental Approach" in Thomas C. Hennessy, ed., *Values and Moral Development* (New York: Paulist, 1976), pp. 173-211, at 175.

24. See Fowler, *Faithful Change*, pp. 47-51, 59, commenting on Ana-Maria Rizzuto, *The Birth of the Living God* (Chicago: University of Chicago Press, 1980).

25. Erikson, "Identity, Psychosocial," p. 61.

26. Erikson, *Childhood and Society*, p. 261.

27. Erikson, *Identity: Youth and Crisis*, pp. 128, 129, 130.

28. Erikson, *Insight and Responsibility*, p. 125 (first quotation in paragraph entirely italicized in original).

29. Erikson, "Life Cycle," p. 290.

30. See Walter E. Conn, "Personal Identity and Creative Self-Understanding: Contributions of Jean Piaget and Erik Erikson to the Psychological Foundations of Theology," *Journal of Psychology and Theology* 5/1 (Winter 1977): 34–39.

31. Erikson, *Insight and Responsibility*, pp. 225, 171, and *Identity: Youth and Crisis*, p. 247.

32. Piaget, *Six Studies*, p. 64.

33. Kegan points out that family and culture hold many expectations of the adolescent: "to be employable, a good citizen, a critical thinker, emotionally self-reflective, personally trustworthy, possessed of common sense and meaningful ideals." All these are aspects of a common expectation that the adolescent "will be able to take out loyalty to or membership in a wider human community than the one defined by...self-interest." This requires that the adolescent give up an "ultimate or absolute relationship" to his or her own point of view (*In Over Our Heads*, pp. 19, 23, 24).

34. Kegan, *In Over Our Heads*, pp. 110, 111. See my consideration of cognitive conversion below in ch. 7 and, much more fully, in ch. 4 of my *Christian Conversion*, from which this chapter draws.
　　In order to indicate how contemporary culture makes demands that require the fourth order consciousness of the Institutional self, Kegan discusses how as parents and partners we are expected to: "1. Take care of the family; establish rules and roles; institute a vision of family purpose. 2. Support the ongoing growth of the young, including their growth within and away from the family. 3. Manage boundaries (inside and outside the family). 4. Set limits on children and on oneself to preserve and protect childhood. 5. Be psychologically independent from, but closely connected to, our spouses. 6. Replace an idealized, romanticized approach to love and closeness with a new conception of love and closeness. 7. Set limits on children, in-laws, oneself, and extrafamily involvements to pre-

serve the couple. 8. Support our partner's development. 9. Communicate well, directly, and fairly. 10. Have an awareness of the way our personal history inclines or directs us" (*In Over Our Heads*, p. 86).

Kegan suggests that "the demands of modern adult life may require a qualitative transformation in the complexity of mind every bit as fundamental as the transformation from magical thinking to concrete thinking required of the school-age child, or the transformation from concrete thinking to abstract thinking required of the adolescent." Put another way, "the mental burden of modern life may be nothing less than the extraordinary cultural demand that each person, in adulthood, create internally an order of consciousness comparable to that which ordinarily would only be found at the level of a community's collective intelligence. This amounts to the expectation that faithful adherents themselves become priests and priestesses; or, that the acculturated become cultures unto themselves" (ibid., p. 134).

35. If women, comfortable at the Interpersonal Stage 3, typically find the transition to Stage 4 difficult, those who do reach Stage 4 may be more open to the transition to Stage 5 than men typically are. Men, though often thought to be most at home in Stage 4, may typically find the transition to Stage 3 difficult and thus tend to get stuck at Stage 2, whose imperialistic individualism can perhaps be confused with genuine Stage 4 independence as easily as Stage 3 fusion is confused with genuine Stage 5 intimacy (a Stage 4 self, remember, has successfully appropriated the interpersonal orientation of Stage 3).

36. Erikson, *Insight and Responsibility*, p. 263.

37. Richard I. Evans, *Dialogue with Erik Erikson* (New York: Dutton, 1969 [1967]), p. 48.

38. Erikson, "Life Cycle," p. 290.

39. Erikson, *Childhood and Society*, p. 263. Erikson's own technical term for "developmental" is "epigenetic."

40. Erikson, *Insight and Responsibility*, pp. 127–28.

41. Erik H. Erikson, "Reflections on the Dissent of Contemporary Youth," *International Journal of Psycho-Analysis* 51 (1970): 11–22, at 16.

42. Kegan, *Evolving Self*, p. 104.

To help distinguish between the Stage 4 self-as-system or self-as-form and the Stage 5 self that transcends system or form, Kegan specifies two related questions: "(1) Do we see the self-as-system as complete and whole or do we regard the self-as-system as incomplete, only a partial construction of all that the self is? (2) Do we identify with the self-as-form (which self then *interacts with* other selves-as-forms) or do we identify with the process of form creation (which brings forms into being and subtends their relationship)?" (*In Over Our Heads,* p. 313). From another angle, we can ask: do we take the self-as-system (form) *as subject* (Stage 4) or do we take it *as object* (Stage 5) (ibid., p. 316)?

43. See Kegan, *Evolving Self,* p. 104. Kegan's distinction between fusion and intimacy may support Erikson against critics who found his identity before intimacy sequence male-centered.

44. Evans, *Dialogue,* p. 51.

45. Erikson, "Life Cycle," p. 291.

46. Erikson, *Insight and Responsibility,* p. 130.

47. Erikson, "Life Cycle," p. 291.

48. See Carol Gilligan, *In a Different Voice: Psychological Theory and Women's Development* (Cambridge: Harvard University Press, 1982) and Walter E. Conn, "Caring Justice—A Conversation," *New Ideas in Psychology* 5/2 (1987): 245-51. For a critique of Gilligan's thesis, see Callahan, "Does Gender Make a Difference in Moral Decision Making?" pp. 67-77. Also see Sidney Callahan, *In Good Conscience: Reason and Emotion in Moral Decision Making* (San Francisco: HarperSanFrancisco, 1991), pp. 195-98.

49. Lawrence Kohlberg and Carol Gilligan, "The Adolescent as a Philosopher: The Discovery of the Self in a Postconventional World," *Daedalus* 100/4 (Fall 1971): 1051-86, at 1068. On how the universal ethical principles of Stage 6 are always related to concrete contexts, see John Michael Murphy and Carol Gilligan, "Moral Development in Late Adolescence and Adulthood: A Critique and Reconstruction of Kohlberg's Theory," *Human Development* 23 (1980): 77-104.

For a valuable consideration of the ethical dimension in pastoral counseling, see Don S. Browning, *The Moral Context of Pastoral Care* (Philadelphia: Westminster, 1976).

50. Fowler, "Stages in Faith," p. 185.

51. See C.G. Jung, "The Stages of Life" and "Psychotherapists or the Clergy" in his *Modern Man in Search of a Soul* (New York: Harcourt, Brace

& World, 1933). Also see Janice Brewi and Anne Brennan, *Mid-Life: Psychological and Spiritual Perspectives* (New York: Crossroad, 1982).

52. Erikson, *Identity: Youth and Crisis,* p. 139.

53. Erikson, "Life Cycle," p. 291. Although the last stage is explicitly designated as religious, the fact is that religion permeates the life cycle from the very beginnings of basic trust. For a helpful guide on this, see Robert C. Fuller, *Religion and the Life Cycle* (Philadelphia: Fortress, 1988).

54. Lawrence Kohlberg, "Education, Moral Development, and Faith," *Journal of Moral Education* 4/1 (1974): 5-16, at 11.

55. Lawrence Kohlberg, "Stages and Aging in Moral Development—Some Speculations," *Gerontologist* 13/4 (Winter 1973): 497-502, at 500.

56. Ibid., pp. 500, 501.

57. James W. Fowler, "Life/Faith Patterns: Structures of Trust and Loyalty" in James W. Fowler and Sam Keen, *Life Maps: Conversations on the Journey of Faith*, ed. Jerome Berryman (Waco, Tex.: Word Books, 1978), pp. 14-101, at 88.

CHAPTER 7

1. For excellent practical reflections on this theme by an experienced director, see William A. Barry, *"Now Choose Life": Conversion as the Way to Life* (New York: Paulist, 1990).

Spiritual direction should not be understood as one person directing another person's spiritual life; rather, the "direction" comes from God's presence and inspiration, which the director assists the directee to notice and respond to. Thus, some prefer the term spiritual "companionship" rather than "direction."

There are many ways to define and relate pastoral counseling and spiritual direction. My approach based on the distinction between development and conversion is offered merely as a suggestion some readers may find helpful, not as a rigid compartmentalization.

For a consideration of some similarities and differences between pastoral counseling and spiritual direction, see Israel Galindo, "Spiritual Direction and Pastoral Counseling: Addressing the Needs of the Spirit," *Journal of Pastoral Care* 51/4 (Winter 1997): 395-402.

2. William James, *The Varieties of Religious Experience* (New York: New

American Library Mentor, 1958 [1902]), pp. 164, 146. For an excellent analysis of conversion from social scientific perspectives, see Lewis R. Rambo, *Understanding Religious Conversion* (New Haven: Yale University Press, 1993).

3. Thomas Merton, *Contemplation in a World of Action* (Garden City, N.Y.: Doubleday Image, 1973 [1971]), p. 225.

4. For his autobiographical account, see Thomas Merton, *The Seven Storey Mountain* (Garden City, N.Y.: Doubleday Image, 1970 [1948]). For helpful guidance on interpreting such autobiographical accounts in terms of genre and historical context, see Karl F. Morrison, *Understanding Conversion* (Charlottesville: University of Virginia Press, 1992), Marjorie O'Rourke Boyle, *Loyola's Acts: The Rhetoric of the Self* (Berkeley: University of California Press, 1997), and Jeffrey D. Martlett, "Conversion Methodology and the Case of Cardinal Newman," *Theological Studies* 58/4 (December 1997): 669-85.

5. For Merton's published diary reflections on this mature experience, see his *The Sign of Jonas* (Garden City, N.Y.: Doubleday Image, 1956 [1953]), *Conjectures of a Guilty Bystander* (Garden City, N.Y.: Doubleday Image, 1968 [1966]), and *The Asian Journal*, ed. N. Burton, P. Hart, and J. Laughlin (New York: New Directions, 1973). Also, after his stipulated twenty-five years past his death (1968), Merton's complete private journals are now being published in seven volumes by HarperSanFrancisco.

6. See Lonergan, *Method in Theology*, pp. 237-43, and "Natural Right and Historical Mindedness," *Proceedings of the American Catholic Philosophical Association* 51 (1977): 132-43, at 140-41.

7. For a detailed interpretation of Merton's youthful conversion as a basic Christian moral conversion, and for expansion on other conversions in a developmental context, see Conn, *Christian Conversion*, from which this chapter draws.

8. Merton, *Seven Storey Mountain*, pp. 184, 203.

9. See Erikson, *Childhood and Society*, pp. 261-63. Also see David D. Cooper's Eriksonian "Young Man Merton: A Speculative Epilogue" in his *Thomas Merton's Art of Denial: The Evolution of a Radical Humanist* (Athens: University of Georgia Press, 1989), pp. 270-91.

10. See Lawrence Kohlberg, *The Psychology of Moral Development* (San Francisco: Harper & Row, 1984), pp. 172-73.

11. See Piaget, *Six Psychological Studies*, pp. 61–64.

12. For excellent biographical and interpretive studies of Merton, see Monica Furlong, *Merton: A Biography* (San Francisco: Harper & Row, 1980); Michael Mott, *The Seven Mountains of Thomas Merton* (Boston: Houghton Mifflin, 1984); John Howard Griffin, *Follow the Ecstasy: The Hermitage Years of Thomas Merton* (Maryknoll, N.Y.: Orbis, 1993 [1983]); Elena Malits, *The Solitary Explorer: Thomas Merton's Transforming Journey* (San Francisco: Harper & Row, 1980); and Anthony T. Padovano, *The Human Journey: Thomas Merton, Symbol of a Century* (Garden City, N.Y.: Doubleday, 1982).

13. See Erikson, *Childhood and Society*, pp. 263–66.

14. Lonergan, *Method in Theology*, p. 105.

15. Merton, *Conjectures of a Guilty Bystander*, p. 157.

16. Cooper, p. 187, quoting Merton, *Contemplation in a World of Action*, p. 227. Also see Griffin, pp. 46–99, esp. 72, 81.

17. See Walter E. Conn, "The Ontogenetic Ground of Value," *Theological Studies* 39/2 (June 1976): 313–35, at 328–35.

Through such conversion of consciousness, writes Kegan, "Our loyalty is transformed from adherence to a value to the process of originating or inventing what is valuable" (*In Over Our Heads*, p. 169).

18. See Walter E. Conn, "Merton's 'True Self': Moral Autonomy and Religious Conversion," *Journal of Religion* 65/4 (October 1985): 513–29.

19. See Merton, *Seven Storey Mountain*, pp. 378–79.

20. See Thomas Merton, *A Search for Solitude*, The Journals of Thomas Merton 3, ed. Lawrence S. Cunningham (San Francisco: HarperSanFrancisco, 1996), pp. 225, 303-4, 309, 313, 319, 330-31, 341-44, 355-56.

21. See Merton, *Conjectures of a Guilty Bystander*, p. 280.

22. See Erikson, *Childhood and Society*, pp. 266–68.

23. See Kohlberg, *Psychology of Moral Development*, pp. 491–96.

24. See Merton, *Seven Storey Mountain*, pp. 376–82.

25. See Thomas Merton, *Dancing in the Water of Life: Seeking Peace in the*

Hermitage, The Journals of Thomas Merton, 5, ed. Robert E. Daggy (San Francisco: HarperSanFrancisco, 1997), p. 204.

26. See Seward Hiltner, "Toward a Theology of Conversion in the Light of Psychology," *Pastoral Psychology* 17 (September 1966): 35-42. For a sociological study of conversion in older adults, see Richard M. Erikson, *Late Have I Loved Thee: Stories of Religious Conversion and Commitment in Later Life* (New York: Paulist, 1995). For a recent and very readable consideration of spiritual search and conversion, see Harry R. Moody and David Carroll, *The Five Stages of the Soul* (New York: Doubleday Anchor, 1997), who distinguish call, search, struggle, breakthrough, and return.

27. See Kohlberg, "Stages and Aging in Moral Development," pp. 500-1.

28. See Erikson, *Childhood and Society*, pp. 268-69. Also see Walter E. Conn, "Adult Conversions," *Pastoral Psychology* 34/4 (1986): 225-36.

29. See Fowler, *Stages of Faith*, p. 198.

30. Lonergan, *Method in Theology*, pp. 240, 242.

31. I articulate religious conversion in this paragraph in Christian theistic terms, but, as the discussion of Kohlberg's "Stage 7" and the preceding paragraph make clear, this articulation is neither necessary nor exclusive.

32. See Conn, "Merton's 'True Self'".

33. Merton, *Conjectures of a Guilty Bystander*, p. 157.

34. Merton, *Asian Journal*, pp. 233-36.

35. Carr, *Search for Wisdom and Spirit*, p. 43, quoting Merton, "Inner Experience," pp. 6-8.

36. Merton, "Inner Experience," pp. 6-8.

37. Carr, p. 43.

38. Thomas Merton, *Zen and the Birds of Appetite* (New York: New Directions, 1968), p. 49.

39. Merton, "Inner Experience," p. 9.

40. Merton, *Zen and the Birds of Appetite*, p. 71.

41. Merton, "Inner Experience," p. 10.

42. Merton, *Zen and the Birds of Appetite*, p. 24.

43. Ibid., pp. 72, 75.

44. George Kilcourse, *Ace of Freedoms: Thomas Merton's Christ* (Notre Dame, Ind.: University of Notre Dame Press, 1993), pp. 212, 219-20.

45. Lonergan, *Method in Theology*, pp. 77, 342.

46. Merton, *Seeds of Contemplation*, p. 41 (entire quotation italicized in original).

47. For a consideration of the true self and false self in Merton's poetry, see Kilcourse, *passim*.

48. See Carr, pp. 106-8.

49. Thomas Merton, "Day of a Stranger" in *A Thomas Merton Reader*, ed. Thomas P. McDonnell (rev. ed.; Garden City, N.Y.: Doubleday Image, 1974 [1962]), p. 434; and Merton, *Conjectures of a Guilty Bystander*, p. 151.

50. See Conn, "Merton's 'True Self.'"

51. The importance given to conversion in the contemporary American Catholic community is seen in the fact that it is promoted both officially by major programs like RENEW and the RCIA (see Robert D. Duggan, ed., *Conversion and the Catechumenate* [New York: Paulist, 1984]) and unofficially by groups like Call to Action (see "Call to Action News," a supplement in the *National Catholic Reporter* 34/11 [16 January 1998]).

CHAPTER 8

1. Fowler, *Stages of Faith*, p. 287.

2. Ibid., p. 288.

3. Ibid.

4. Ibid., p. 289.

5. See ibid., p. 290.

6. See ibid., p. 264.

7. Ibid.

8. Ibid., p. 265.

9. Indeed, Jung's self may be more heuristic than actual, a goal of individuating development rather than a presently existing reality, as Ford-Grabowsky seems to make it.

10. Ford-Grabowsky, "Flaws in Faith Development Theory," p. 85.

11. See ibid., pp. 85, 86.

12. Fowler, *Faithful Change*, p. 20.

13. James W. Fowler, "Faith Development Theory and the Aims of Religious Socialization" in Gloria Durka and Joan-Marie Smith, eds., *Emerging Issues in Religious Education* (New York: Paulist, 1976), pp. 187–211, at 199, 200.

14. Ibid., p. 200.

15. Fowler, *Stages of Faith*, p. 260.

16. James, *Psychology: The Briefer Course*, p. 47.

17. Fowler, *Stages of Faith*, p. 258.

18. Ibid., pp. 259, 260.

19. Ibid., pp. 261, 262.

20. Ibid., p. 263.

21. Ibid., p. 281; on structure/content distinction, see ibid., pp. 249, 272.

22. Ibid., pp. 281–82 (entire quotation italicized in original).

23. See ibid., pp. 276–77, 282, 275, 285–86.

24. Ibid., pp. 287, 287–88.

25. Ibid., pp. 290, 291.

26. See, e.g., Ford-Grabowsky, "Flaws," p. 83.

27. See Conn, *Christian Conversion*, p. 27.

28. Further, a focus on conversion as structural change takes account of Ford-Grabowsky's point ("Flaws," p. 85) that the meaning of development

in Fowler's theory is not univocal. This focus makes it clear that there is an explicit existential as well as an implicit natural dimension in normative stage development (see Conn, *Christian Conversion*, pp. 110-16).

29. An exception to her uncritical pattern may be Mary's criticism of the deception, arrogance, and brainwashing she found in the Followers of God, her first Christian community, but this may be better explained as issuing from her stubborn counterdependent stance.

30. Fowler, *Stages of Faith*, p. 221.

31. See, e.g., ibid., p. 226.

32. See Ford-Grabowsky, "Flaws," p. 89.

APPENDIX

1. See Gerard Egan, *The Skilled Helper* (Monterey, Cal.: Brooks/Cole, 1982).

2 See Gerald Corey, *Theory and Practice of Counseling and Psychotherapy* (Monterey, Cal.: Brooks/Cole, 1982).

3. These two phases in Stage 2 may be distinguished in terms of subject-pole (first) and object-pole (second). In spiritual direction, discernment focuses especially on the subject-pole, on prayerfully understanding the self under God's guidance (see, e.g., the classic "Rules for the Discernment of Spirits" in the *Spiritual Exercises* of Ignatius of Loyola). For specific decision making leading to concrete action at the object-pole, spiritual directors will also need to help directees with some methodical approach (see, e.g., the ethical method presented in Daniel C. Maguire, *The Moral Choice* [Garden City, N.Y. Doubleday, N.Y. 1978]).

INDEX

Included from notes, in addition to terms from substantive discussions, are authors of articles and books as well as editors of books which have no designated author. In cases of multiple authors or editors, the name of the first is included. The term "self" appears only in its compound forms.